T0161572

THE COMINTERN

THE COMINTERN

A History of the Third International

DUNCAN HALLAS

Haymarket Books
Chicago, Illinois

First published in Great Britain in 1985 by Bookmarks
©1985 Duncan Hallas

This edition published in 2008 by Haymarket Books
P.O. Box 180165, Chicago, IL 60618
www.haymarketbooks.org
773-583-7884

ISBN 978-1-93185-952-3

Distributed to the trade in the US through Consortium Book
Sales and Distribution (www.cbsd.com) and internationally
through Ingram Publisher Services International
(www.ingramcontent.com).

This book was published with the generous support of Lannan
Foundation and Wallace Action Fund.

Special discounts re available for bulk purchases by
organizations and institutions. Please call 773-583-7884 or
email info@haymarketbooks.org for more information.

Printed in the United States.

Entered into digital printing November 2019.

CONTENTS

INTRODUCTION
TO THE
1985 EDITION

IN JANUARY 1918 Lenin wrote: "We are far from having completed even the transitional period from capitalism to socialism. We have never cherished the hope that we could finish it without the aid of the international proletariat. We have never had any illusions on that score.... The final victory of socialism in a single country is of course impossible."[1]

In July of the same year he repeated:

> We never harbored the illusion that the forces of the proletariat and the revolutionary people of one country, however heroic and however organized and disciplined they might be, could overthrow international imperialism. That can be done only by the joint effort of the workers of the world.[2]

And again, in March 1919:

> Complete and final victory...cannot be achieved in Russia alone; it can be achieved only when the proletariat is victorious in at least all the advanced countries, or, at all events, in some of the largest of the advanced countries. Only then shall we be able to say with absolute confidence that the cause of the proletariat has triumphed, that our first objective—the overthrow of capitalism—has been achieved.[3]

Internationalism is the bedrock of socialism, not simply or mainly for sentimental reasons but because capitalism has created a world economy that can be transformed only on a world scale. Anything else is utopianism. The Communist International, which arose out of the Russian Revolution of October 1917, was not an optional extra but an essential, indispensable part of that revolution, which, in turn, was part of an international revolutionary upheaval.

Conversely, the events that were to follow ten years later, turning the Comintern—as it had come to be known—into a tool of Russian foreign policy, were part of the strangling of workers' power inside the USSR by the rising bureaucracy under Stalin. There is an enormous amount of literature about the Comintern, the Third or Communist International. Some is Stalinist; more is social democratic; and most is the output of various U.S. universities, promoted by the CIA in the interests of U.S. foreign policy—and doubtless much of this is CIA-financed too. There is, of course, some serious academic writing on the subject, but there is no account of the Comintern written in English from a revolutionary socialist point of view.

Or rather there is no easily available account. Two books— C. L. R. James's *World Revolution*, published in 1936, and K. Tilak's *Rise and Fall of the Comintern* (1947)—made a start in this direction. Both are inadequate and both are, for practical purposes, unobtainable. Claudin's *The Communist Movement* (1975) is informative but politically weak, where not downright bad. This small book aims to provide, from a revolutionary socialist point of view, an introduction to the Comintern, from its founding conference in 1919 to its winding-up by Stalin in 1943.

In 1932, Trotsky, then a powerless and persecuted exile from the USSR, wrote a statement that was intended to serve as a political basis for an international left opposition to the Communist Parties under Stalin. In it he wrote:

> The International Left Opposition stands on the ground of the first four congresses of the Comintern. This does not mean that it bows before every letter of its decisions, many of which had a purely conjunctional character and have been contradicted by subsequent events. But all the essential principles (in relation to imperialism and the bourgeois state; to democracy and reformism; problems of insurrection; the dictatorship of the proletariat; on relations with the peasantry and the oppressed nations; soviets; work in the trade unions; parliamentarianism; the policy of the united front) remain even today the highest expression of proletarian strategy in the epoch of the general crisis of capitalism.[4]

The Socialist Workers Party, in Britain, also stands on this ground—which is why the emphasis of this book is on the

Comintern's revolutionary period, the period of the first four congresses and immediately after.

I am greatly indebted to Nigel Harris, who persuaded me to write the book, to Tony Cliff, who subjected the first draft to a severe and valuable criticism, and to Alex Callinicos, Peter Goodwin, Peter Marsden, Steve Pepper, Dave Sherry, Ahmed Sehrawy, and Steve Wright, who all contributed to its final shape, although I have not always followed their advice.

Duncan Hallas
April 1985

ONE

THE BEGINNINGS

"Sweeping aside the halfheartedness, lies, and corruptions of the outlived official Socialist Parties, we Communists, united in the Third International, consider ourselves the direct continuation of the heroic endeavors and martyrdom of a long line of revolutionary generations from Babeuf to Karl Liebknecht and Rosa Luxemburg.... Our task is to generalize the revolutionary experiences of the working class, to cleanse the movement of the disintegrating admixture of opportunism and social patriotism, to mobilize the forces of all genuinely revolutionary parties of the world working class, and thereby facilitate and hasten the victory of the communist revolution throughout the world."
Manifesto of the First Congress of the Third International, 1919

MARCH 4, 1919. Thirty-five delegates meeting in the Kremlin voted, with one abstention, to constitute the Third or Communist International—soon to be known as the Comintern. It was not a particularly weighty or representative gathering. Only the five delegates from the Russian Communist Party (Bukharin, Chicherin, Lenin, Trotsky, and Zinoviev) represented a party that was both a mass organization and a genuinely revolutionary one.

Stange of the Norwegian Labor Party (DNA) came from a mass party, but, as events were to prove, the DNA was far from revolutionary in practice. Hugo Eberlein of the newly formed Communist Party of Germany (KPD) represented a real revolutionary organization but one that was still only a few thousand strong. Most of the other delegates represented very little, often nothing, since their presence in Moscow was accidental.

On these grounds, Eberlein, acting on the instructions of the KPD central committee, wished to confine the meeting to preliminary work, to the adoption of a provisional program and so on. Western Europe, he noted, was entirely unrepresented. The common view that what the Germans really feared was undue Russian dominance is probably correct but this argument was not openly advanced.

The delegates took it for granted that an "International" without some real mass support in a number of countries was nonsense. Zinoviev, for the Russians, argued that mass support existed in fact. The weakness of many of the delegations was accidental, he said. "We have a victorious workers' revolution in a great country.... You have in Germany a party marching to power which in a few months will establish a working-class government. And are we still to delay? No one will understand it."[1]

That the socialist revolution was an immediate prospect in central Europe, above all in Germany, was doubted by none of the delegates. Eberlein himself had said, "Unless all the signs are deceptive, the German proletariat is facing the last decisive struggle. However difficult it may be, the prospects for communism are favorable."[2] Lenin, the most sober and calculating of revolutionaries, had said in his opening speech that "not only in Russia but in the most developed capitalist countries of Europe, Germany for example, civil war is a fact...the world revolution is beginning and growing in intensity everywhere."[3]

This was not fantasy. In November 1918, the German Empire, until then the most powerful state in Europe, had collapsed under the impact of a mass revolution. Six people's commissars, three of them Social Democrats and three Independent Social Democrats, replaced the Kaiser's government. Workers' and soldiers' councils had sprung up throughout Germany and wielded effective power. True, the Social Democratic leaders, who dominated these councils, bent all their efforts to reconstituting the old capitalist state power under a new "republican" guise. That was all the more reason for creating a revolutionary International of socialist organizations with a strong centralized leadership to guide and support the struggle for a Soviet Germany—one in which the reins of power would be held by workers' councils or soviets, to use their Russian name.

And that struggle, in spite of the bloody suppression of the Spartakus rising in January 1919, appeared to be going forward. "From January to May 1919, with offshoots reaching into the height of the summer, a bloody civil war was waged in Germany…"[4] A month after the Moscow meeting, the Bavarian Soviet Republic was proclaimed.

The other great central European power, the Austro-Hungarian Empire, had ceased to exist. The revolutionary risings of late 1918 had pulled it apart. Its successor states themselves were in varying degrees of revolutionary ferment. In German-speaking Austria, the only effective armed force was the Volkswehr (People's Army), controlled by the Social Democrats. In Hungary, a Soviet Republic was formed on March 21. All the new or reconstituted states, Czechoslovakia, Yugoslavia, even Poland, were unstable.

The role of the leaders of socialist parties in all these countries was crucial. These parties called themselves "Social Democrats." The Russian Bolsheviks had originally been the consistently revolutionary wing of the Russian Social Democratic Party. But the other Social Democratic parties in Europe were now far from revolutionary. The majority in fact supported counterrevolution in the name of "democracy." Most of them claimed to be, indeed once had been, Marxists and internationalists. They were now a major prop of capitalism, using socialist phrases and the credit established by their years of agitation to *prevent* the establishment of workers' power, or to prevent its consolidation where it was temporarily established.

Their attempt to reconstitute the Second International by a meeting at Berne in Switzerland was advanced as a further, urgent reason for proclaiming the Third. As early as 1914, Lenin had written, "the Second International is dead, overcome by opportunism…long live the Third International."[5] Now, eighteen months after the October Revolution in Russia, the call for a new International could be turned into a reality. It had taken five years—years of war, deepening social crisis, massive workers' struggles, and revolutions—to create the conditions necessary for a real revolutionary International to be born.

Social democracy in 1914

"If the outbreak of war threatens, it is the duty of the workers and their parliamentary representatives in the countries involved, with the aid of the International Socialist Bureau, to exert all their efforts to prevent the war by means of coordinated action. If war nevertheless breaks out, it is their duty to work for its speedy end, and to exploit with all their forces the economic and political crisis created by the war to arouse the population and to hasten the overthrow of capitalist class rule."

Resolution of the Stuttgart Congress of the Second
International, 1907

THE SECOND International had been founded at a congress in Paris that opened, symbolically, on July 14, 1889—the centenary of the storming of the Bastille, which had marked the outbreak of the great French Revolution. It proclaimed itself the heir of the International Working Men's Association (1864–72) in which Karl Marx himself had played a leading role.

> The Salle Petrelle, where the congress took place, was festooned with red cloth, reinforced by red flags. Above the rostrum, in gold letters, shone the closing words of the *Communist Manifesto*, "Working men of all countries unite!" An inscription in the foreground announced the central aim in the fight for working-class emancipation: "Political and Economic Expropriation of the Capitalist Class...." The spirit of the French [hosts] was admirably expressed on a poster at the rostrum.... "In the name of the Paris of June 1848, and of March, April and May 1871, of the France of Babeuf, Blanqui and Varlin, greetings to the Socialist workers of both worlds." After the congress was over the delegates organized a march in honor of the revolutionary pioneers.[6]

Founded under these seemingly revolutionary auspices, the Second International served as a focus around which grew some large workers' parties that commonly took as their name "social democratic party"—a term that Marx himself had disliked, preferring "communist." They were not by any means the only workers' parties, but they were the ones that dominated the workers' movement in the years up to the First World War.

Social democracy, in the classical sense, had a fairly short life. The German Social Democratic Party (SPD), the model for the rest, "the pillar and example," was founded in 1875. It adopted what was then regarded as a Marxist program (the Erfurt program) in 1891. Between 1878 and 1890, the SPD had been an illegal organization, proscribed by Bismarck's antisocialist law. "At the first congress in exile (Wyden, Switzerland, 1880), it unanimously voted to strike from its program the clause stating that it would pursue its aims by 'all legal means.' During this time of troubles, the urban working class became increasingly alienated from the state."[7] This was demonstrated by voting figures. The SPD was outlawed, but socialist candidates (in fact SPD nominees) were able to contest elections. On a restricted suffrage, they polled, collectively, some 300,000 votes in 1881 and one and a half million in 1890. By 1912, the party, now a legally tolerated but socially outlawed organization, polled four and a quarter million votes (34 percent of the total poll) and elected 110 deputies to the Reichstag (the German federal parliament). In 1914, the SPD had 1,086,000 card-holding members.

In France, the unified socialist party (SFIO: French Section of the Workers' International), founded in 1905, gained 102 seats in the elections held early in 1914. A year earlier, the Italian Socialist Party (PSI) had gained a quarter of the vote cast and 78 deputies. The Austro-Hungarian party had won more than a million votes and 82 deputies. From Scandinavia to the Balkans, Marxist social democratic parties gained members, votes, and deputies. Even in the United States the Socialist Party (founded in 1901) had, by 1912, 125,000 members and won 800,000 votes, having "56 mayors, 160 councilmen and 145 aldermen...eight foreign-language and five English dailies.... In addition, there were 262 English and 36 foreign language weeklies."[8] Weaker but significant movements were growing up everywhere from Britain and Chile to Spain, Switzerland, and Uruguay, all of them affiliated to the Second International and apparently committed to the socialist reconstruction of society and to uncompromising opposition to "national unity" and war.

It was an illusion. There were considerable differences among the various social democratic parties but basically they were pseudo-revolutionary parties (the Australian and British Labor Parties and the Socialist Party in the United States were exceptional in lacking Marxist rhetoric and revolutionary pretensions).

They combined an uncompromising verbal hostility to capitalism with a practical activity that was essentially confined to winning members and votes. Because they were excluded from any share of state power, and because they had an ideology that rejected all the values of official society, the social democrats created, to some degree, a whole world of their own. "No German town was without its social democratic daily paper, its consumer cooperative, its workers' sports and cultural associations."[9]

This impressive apparatus had become an end in itself. There was no real perspective that the achievement of socialism would need a struggle for power. Socialism would come inevitably, as a result of the contradictions of capitalism, it was constantly stressed. Confrontation with the forces of the state, or even the employers, was avoided wherever possible. As a political force, social democracy was essentially passive. Though some of the parties, notably the Belgians and the Austrians, had been willing to use—and had used—mass political strikes, this was for the strictly limited purpose of winning or extending the right to vote. Most of the parties would not even go as far as this.

In August 1914, the illusion was destroyed. Social democracy collapsed. The combination of extreme verbal radicalism with political passivity in practice was no longer possible for mass parties in the warring states. The party leaders were faced with a simple choice: maintain their political position, their internationalism, which meant opposing the war, and face a return to illegality, persecution, prison, and the seizure of their massive assets, or abandon all they had stood for in principle, support "their own" imperialist state and gain an honored and increasingly important role in capitalist society. They capitulated and became recruiting sergeants for the First World War. The importance of this collapse cannot be overstressed. Since August 4, 1914, the social democratic parties have acted within the workers' movement as agents for the ruling class.

There were exceptions. The Italians and Americans were not compelled to choose immediately, since their ruling classes remained for a while neutral in the war. The Scandinavians and the Dutch were in this position until 1919. On the other hand, the Serbs, heroically, stood their ground and were subjected to a murderous prosecution. The Bulgarian majority party, which had split from its right-wing minority in 1903, opposed the war. In Russia, the Bolsheviks, and even some of the Mensheviks, refused to support the tsarist war machine. Everywhere else, those who opposed the war were in a minority.

Karl Liebknecht, the SPD deputy who at first stood alone against the war in the German Reichstag, wrote: "Every people's main enemy is in their own country! The main enemy of the German people is in Germany. German imperialism, the German war party and German secret diplomacy—here in our own land is the enemy that the German people must combat. We must wage this political struggle alongside the proletariat of other countries, as they struggle against their own imperialists.... Down with the warmongers on both sides of the border.... The main enemy is at home."[10]

But the "social patriots," as their opponents soon came to call the social democrats who supported the war, were able to claim that, in 1914, they had the support of the mass of politically conscious workers. It was true. Trotsky noted that in Vienna "the patriotic enthusiasm of the masses in Austria-Hungary seemed especially surprising."

What was it that drew them? he asked.

> What sort of an idea? The national idea? But Austria-Hungary was the very negation of any national idea. No, the moving force was something different. The people whose lives, day in and day out, pass in a monotony of hopelessness are many.... The alarm of mobilization breaks into their lives like a promise.... Changes still more incredible are in store.... For better or worse? For the better of course—what can seem worse than "normal" conditions?...War affects everybody and those who are oppressed and deceived by life consequently feel that they are on an equal footing with the rich and powerful."[11]

Similarly in London, Paris, and Berlin, there was mass enthusiasm for the war.

But revolutionaries who cannot withstand temporary popular hatred, as well as official persecution, are worthless. The pioneers of social democracy had withstood both in their time. Why did they betray their own past?

One explanation is that they did not, that after the Stuttgart congress of 1907, the major parties moved rapidly to the right, toward support for "their own" imperialist ruling classes. Of course it is true that opportunist trends were growing inside these parties, that active right-wing tendencies, recovering from

their defeat at the turn of the century on the issues of cooperation with the "progressive" bourgeois parties and participation
in "progressive" bourgeois governments, were raising their
heads again.

None of this, however, can weaken the force of the accusa-
tion of betrayal, can alter *the fact* of betrayal. For the Extraordinary Congress of Basel, held in 1912 specifically to deal with
the increasing danger of imperialist war, *unanimously* reiterated and strengthened the Stuttgart resolution against war.

As Zinoviev, then Lenin's closest collaborator, wrote in 1916:

> The Basel manifesto was written in anticipation of precisely *the
> very Europe-wide war* that has now broken out.... It laid out a
> program of action for the socialists of all nations. What kind of
> program? Does it contain the slightest suggestion that the So-
> cialists of even one of the countries that will be dragged into the
> war will have to "defend the fatherland" and apply the criterion
> of "defensive war?" No. *Not a word, not a murmur of this!*
> You find in it an appeal to organize civil war, and references to
> the Paris Commune, to the 1905 Revolution, and so forth. But
> you will *not* find in it a single thing about "defensive" war. The
> Basel resolution was not worse, but better than that of
> Stuttgart. Every word in it is a slap in the face to the present tac-
> tics of the "leading" parties of the Second International."[12]

This is substantially true. Indeed the major opposition on
this issue at the successive congresses came from those such as
James Keir Hardie of the British Labor Party, who wished to
commit the parties of the Second International to call an immediate general strike on the outbreak of war!

Another explanation is the fatalistic character of social democratic theory. Karl Kautsky, "the pope of Marxism" and
chief theoretician of the SPD, put it in these words: "The Socialist Party is a revolutionary party but not a revolution-mak-
ing party. We know that our goal can be attained only through
revolution. We also know that it is just as little in our power to
create this revolution as it is in the power of our opponents to
prevent it."[13] A fine theoretical justification for passivity! The
idea that socialists must win workers *in struggle* is entirely
missing. And not by accident.

According to Marx, practice comes before theory. "In the beginning was the deed." The theory of a mass movement has *material* as well as intellectual roots. Near the end of his life, John

Wesley, the founder of Methodism, wrote, in a remarkable antic-
ipation of the materialist conception of history: "The Methodists
in every place grow diligent and frugal; consequently they increase in goods. Hence they proportionally increase...in the desire of the flesh...and in the pride of life. So, although the form
of religion remains, the spirit is swiftly vanishing away."[14]
    So it was with social democracy. A whole layer of social de-
mocrats had prospered. By 1913, the SPD and its associated
trade unions owned property worth ninety million marks. To
administer and control it, "the party had generated a whole category of parliamentarians, working-class bureaucrats and functionaries in the unions, the cooperatives, the party secretariats,
the editorial offices of the party press.... Such people no longer
lived for, but also off the working-class movement."[15]
    They had a great deal more to lose than their chains.
    Lenin emphasized another fundamental material factor.
"Opportunism was engendered in the course of decades by the
special features in this period of the development of capitalism,
when the comparatively peaceful and cultured life of a stratum
of privileged working men "bourgeoisified" them, gave them
crumbs from the table of their national capitalists."[16] This
"labor aristocracy" theory, which had earlier been developed
by Marx himself in the special case of Britain, contained an important kernel of truth.
    But it was to prove an oversimplification. Skilled (and
"privileged") workers played an important part in the antiwar
movement. That movement began to grow as the casualty lists
and economic hardship grew, and both grew massively after
1915 in all the main warring states.
    Nevertheless, the revolutionary left, a few "ultralefts"
apart, underestimated the role of the *labor bureaucracies* as a
distinct social layer. This is a matter to which we will return.

The rising tide

*"The imperialist war is ushering in the era of the social revolu-
tion. All the objective conditions of recent times have put the
workers' revolutionary mass struggle on the order of the day. It is
the duty of socialists, while making every use of every means of
the working class's legal struggle, to...develop the workers' revo-*

lutionary consciousness…promote and encourage any revolutionary action, and do everything possible to turn the imperialist war between peoples into a civil war…for the conquest of political power by the working class, and the realization of socialism."
Resolution of the Zimmerwald Left, 1915

THE OUTBREAK of the world war seemed, at first, to have split the socialist movement into two parts, the "social patriots," who were the great majority, and the "internationalists." It soon became obvious, however, that the movement was really split into three. The internationalists themselves were divided between consistent revolutionaries and what came to be called the "center."

The centrists took a pacifist or semi-pacifist position. They were against support for "their own" governments and in favor of a negotiated peace. They wanted to reconstitute international links between the socialist parties, illegally if need be in the case of the best of them, but looked back to a rebirth of the old International rather than the building of a new revolutionary International. They saw the war as a disastrous interruption of "normal" political life, not as an opportunity for socialist revolution. For them, the International was for "peacetime," for May Day speeches, not for revolutionary struggle to change the world.

In September 1915, the Italian and Swiss parties succeeded in convening a conference of antiwar socialists at Zimmerwald, near Berne in Switzerland. Both these parties were dominated by the "center." The Swiss were neutral (although both pro-French and pro-German tendencies existed in the party), and the majority of the Italians, the PSI, maintained a centrist antiwar position even after Italy's entry into the war in May 1915. Not many came to the conference. "The delegates themselves joked about the fact that half a century after the founding of the first International, it was possible to seat all the internationalists in four coaches."[17]

At Zimmerwald, the split between the centrists and the left came into the open. As well as the two sponsoring parties there were German, French, Swedish, Norwegian, Dutch, Polish, Russian, and other delegates present. By nineteen votes to twelve, the conference rejected the draft resolution submitted by Lenin that contained the call to "turn the imperialist war into a civil war." In spite of this, Lenin called the conference "the first step" and the left, including the Bolsheviks, voted for the manifesto of the majority as well as publishing their own rejected resolution. "The capitalists of all countries claim that the war serves to defend the fatherland.... They are lying," declared the manifesto.

"It is a fact that this manifesto is a step forward towards a real struggle against opportunism, towards a rupture with it," wrote Lenin. In spite of its "inconsistency and timidity," he said, "it would be sectarianism to refuse to take this step forward."[18] In the atmosphere of frenzied "patriotism" that still existed in 1915, when any contact with "enemy" nationals was regarded as treason, Zimmerwald was indeed a real step forward for socialist internationalism.

At the next conference, at Kienthal (also in Switzerland) in 1916, the left took a harder line. "Every step forward taken by the international labor movement along the road mapped out by Zimmerwald shows more and more clearly the inconsistency of the position adopted by the Zimmerwald majority," declared another unsuccessful Bolshevik resolution. The Zimmerwald majority, said the resolution, "is afraid of a break with the International Socialist Bureau [the Second International's completely inactive center].... It is the social chauvinists and Kautskyites of all countries who will undertake the task of restoring the bankrupt International Socialist Bureau. The task of socialists is to explain to the masses the inevitability of a split with those who pursue a bourgeois policy under the flag of socialism."[19] This was a call for a *political* break not only with the right but with the fake left, those who supported pacifism and saw negotiation between the warring powers as the way to end the war.

By this time, the antiwar movements were gaining some real support. Easter 1916 saw the Dublin rising against British imperialism. Karl Liebknecht and Otto Rühle, elected as Reichstag deputies for the SPD, had broken with the SPD and were agitating in the Reichstag against the war. In May 1916, the arrest of Karl Liebknecht for treason provoked a strike by fifty thousand workers in Berlin and a wave of clashes with the police. The shop stewards' movement was gaining ground in Britain.

The February 1917 revolution in Russia sparked off massive peace demonstrations in Britain as well as in Germany and Austria-Hungary. That spring the SPD split and the centrists, including the SPD Reichstag leader of 1914, Hugo Haase, and the theoretician Karl Kautsky, founded the Independent Social Democratic Party (USPD) on an antiwar program. However, the split was forced by the SPD right wing, and the antiwar platform was pacifistic, not revolutionary. The USPD was a mishmash of reformists, centrists, and some revolutionaries. The USPD *reflected* growing opposition to the war among German workers; it did not lead it.

The October Revolution in Russia had an even greater effect throughout Europe. In January 1918, mass strikes developed in Austria-Hungary and Germany, strikes not for money but for peace.

> It started at the factory of Manfred Weiss, in Csepel, near Budapest, by far the biggest munitions factory in Hungary…. The strike spread like wildfire…. By the 16th of January it had reached the munitions factories of lower Austria; on the 17th all Vienna went on strike. A few days later the Berlin munitions workers followed suit, and then the engineers and many other branches of industry all over the Reich. Nowhere had the official leadership called the strike…. The movement shook the Central Powers to their very foundations.[20]

More than two million workers were involved, but the movement was contained. Like the big mutinies in the French Army in 1917, it lacked a coherent revolutionary leadership.

But the mutiny of the sailors of the German High Seas fleet at Kiel on November 4, 1918, led to the collapse of imperial Germany.

> In Kiel there was only one authority—the council of workers', sailors', and soldiers' deputies…. From Kiel the rebellion spread to Hamburg and on the night of November 8th it was learned in Berlin that it had triumphed, with little or no resistance, in Hanover, Magdeburg, Cologne, Munich, Stuttgart, Frankfurt-am-Main, Brunswick, Oldenburg, Wittenberg, and other cities.[21]

On November 9, the especially "reliable" Fourth Regiment of Fusiliers was rushed into Berlin. It mutinied. The Kaiser fled to Holland. The German workers' and soldiers' councils were in power.

The point needs emphasizing. They were *in power:* no other authority in Germany disposed of an effective armed force. The betrayal of this *successful* movement by the leaders of the SPD (and the USPD) in the name of "democracy" now deepened the split of 1914. The issue of whether authority should lie with workers' councils or parliament was now central.

Democracy and dictatorship

"Democracy assumed different forms and was applied in different degrees in the ancient republics of Greece, the medieval cities and the advanced capitalist countries. It would be sheer nonsense to think that the most profound revolution in history, the first case in the history of the world of power being transferred from the exploiting minority to the exploited majority, could take place within the time-worn framework of the old, bourgeois parliamentary democracy, without drastic changes, without the creation of new forms of democracy, new institutions that embody the new conditions for applying democracy."

Resolution of the First Congress of the Communist International, 1919

SOVIETS OR parliament? After the October Revolution, the Russian Communist Party had dispersed the newly elected Constituent Assembly, in which the right wing of the Social Revolutionary Party, nominally a peasant party, had a majority, and had chosen in favor of handing power to the soviets of workers', soldiers', and peasants' delegates. After the November Revolution, the German Social Democratic Party had dissolved the workers' and soldiers' councils, in which it had a majority, in favor of the National Assembly in which it did not. True, the SPD leaders were compelled to support a (unanimous) motion calling for the abolition of the standing army and the arming of the workers—but this was mere deception.

In both cases, the question of constitutional forms was really a question of class power. The effect of the Russian Communist Party's action was to create a workers' state. The effect of the SPD's action in Germany was to create a reconstituted bourgeois state, the Weimar Republic. Marx had written, after the Paris Commune, that the form of state in the transition from capitalism to socialism, "can only be the revolutionary dictatorship of the proletariat." The SPD leadership declared, during the November Revolution: "All power to the Councils of Workers' and Soldiers' Deputies? No. We reject the idea of the dictatorship of one class if the majority of the people are not behind that class."[22]

The social democrats had come, in practice, to reject the essence of the Marxist theory of the state: that the state is "merely the organized power of one class for oppressing another," that all states are class states, that there is no such thing as a "neutral" state. They had done more. They had come to reject their own previous position that socialist revolution was inevitable and had turned in favor of "peaceful," parliamentary roads to socialism.

Yet the Weimar Republic was every bit as much a product of the violent overthrow of the previous state as the Russian Soviet Republic. Mutinous soldiers and armed workers, not voters, overthrew the German Empire. The same was true of the successor states of Austria-Hungary. The revolution had come, in spite of the social democrats. Now they bent all their efforts to restoring the bourgeois state. The greater transformation, the destruction of capitalism, was, according to the social democratic right, to be achieved by the ordinary mechanisms of bourgeois democracy, once the bourgeois state had been restored complete with its army and police!

In fact, this meant the abandonment of socialism. It was politically and psychologically impossible for the SPD leadership to admit this in 1919. When finally it did so, forty years later at the Bad Godesberg conference in 1959, it was merely drawing the logical conclusions from its actions in 1914 and 1919. Theory was at last brought into line with practice.

The Third International, in its 1919 *Platform*, sharply restated the Marxist position. "The victory of the working class lies in shattering the organization of the enemy power and organizing workers' power; it consists in the destruction of the bourgeois state machine and the construction of the workers' state machine."[23] There could be no question of socialism through parliament. Lenin, in 1917, had quoted with approval Engels's statement that universal suffrage is "an index of the maturity of the working class. It cannot and never will be anything more in the modern state."[24] "No bourgeois republic, however democratic," he wrote just after the Moscow conference, "ever was or could have been anything but a machine for the repression of the working people by capital, an instrument of the dictatorship of the bourgeoisie, the political rule of capital."[25]

The workers' republic, based on workers' councils, was truly democratic. "The essence of soviet power lies in this, that the permanent and sole foundation of the entire state power, of the entire state apparatus, is the mass organization of those very classes which were oppressed by the capitalists, that is, the workers and semi-workers (peasants who do not exploit labor...)"[26] This was something of an idealization of Russia, even in 1919, but the "deviations" were accounted for by the backwardness of the country and the still-raging civil war and foreign intervention. The subsequent victory of Stalinism enabled the social democrats to obscure the reality—that workers' power means rule by workers' own organizations. Without democracy *within* those organizations, the workers cannot rule. Equally, without the dominance of those organizations institutionalized through a workers' state, the workers cannot rule.

It is not today only or even mainly the social democrats who lie about this, although they pioneered the original misrepresentation in the 1920s. Two immensely powerful ruling groups have a vital vested interest in burying the notion that workers' councils, soviets, a workers' republic, a soviet republic, mean the actual producers of the things we all need collectively and democratically determining the conditions of their work and life and shaping the whole of society accordingly.

These are on the one hand the small clique of top bureaucrats who run the USSR, together with their allies, satellites, and imitators, and, even more so, the ruling class of the United States, with their allies, satellites, and ideologists. These people habitually refer to "the Soviets" doing this or that. Actually there are no soviets in Russia and have been none since the early 1920s. The "Supreme Soviet" and other bodies in the USSR that are given the name of soviet are in no way organs of workers' power as they were set up by the revolutionary workers of 1917. It suits the interests of the bureaucratic rulers of the USSR, however, to maintain the fiction—their claim to the inheritance of the workers' revolution of 1917 is used to validate their rule *over* the workers. It also suits the interests of the ruling classes of the West to identify soviets, workers' power, with their opposite—bureaucratic dictatorship over the working class. Unfortunately many on the left are also willing to accept, in varying degrees, this ideological framework promoted by Moscow and Washington alike. Of course, there was none of this in March 1919.

The delegates meeting in Moscow had constituted the new International on the basis of uncompromising internationalism, a decisive and final split with the traitors of 1914, workers' power, workers' councils, the defense of the Russian Soviet Republic, and the perspective of revolution in the near future in Central and Western Europe. The problem now was to create the mass parties that could make all this a reality.

The means lay at hand. Centrist leaders such as those who called the Zimmerwald conference controlled the Italian party and were soon to capture the French. The German USPD was soon to have eight hundred thousand members. Everywhere in Europe big centrist movements were developing as a result of a big influx of workers radicalized by seeing the horrors of world war. Their members had to be won for communism.

The foundations had been laid. The struggle against the centrist leaders was now the major immediate task. And a very urgent one. For mass "centrist" organizations (as opposed to small groups) are inherently unstable. Vacillating as they do between consistent reformist politics and consistent revolutionary politics, they are a typical product of large-scale radicalization such as that which followed the First World War. But they are a *temporary* one. As Trotsky wrote: "The masses don't ever stay for very long in this transitional stage: temporarily they rally to the centrists, then they go on and join the communists or go back to the reformists—unless they lapse into indifference."[27]

THE MASS PARTIES

*"Parties and groups only recently affiliated to the Second Inter-
national are more and more frequently applying for membership
in the Third International, though they have not become really
communist.... The Communist International is, to a certain extent, becoming fashionable.... In certain circumstances, the
Communist International may be faced with the danger of dilu-
tion by the influx of wavering and irresolute groups that have
not yet broken with their Second International ideology."*
Lenin, "The Terms of Admission into the Communist
International," 1920

IN MARCH 1919, the executive of the Italian Socialist Party
(PSI) voted to recommend that the party affiliate to the Third
International. In September, the Bologna congress of the party
voted to affiliate by a large majority. The PSI was a big and growing organization. In the elections of November 1919, it got one-
third of the total vote and returned 156 deputies. The Norwegian
party, the DNA, confirmed its affiliation and the Bulgarian, Yugoslav (formerly Serbian), and Romanian parties joined as well.

The first three of these were important organizations. The
DNA, which was based on trade union affiliation like its
British counterpart, completely dominated the Norwegian left.
The Bulgarian Communist Party had the support, from the be-
ginning, of virtually the whole Bulgarian working class. The
Yugoslavian Communist Party returned fifty-four deputies in
the first (and only) free elections held in the new state.

In France the SFIO, which had more than doubled its membership from ninety thousand in 1914 to two hundred thou-

sand in 1919, had swung far to the left, and was flirting with Moscow. Its leadership really wanted to reconstruct the international movement on a "Zimmerwald majority" basis, excluding out-and-out social patriots such as the leaders of the British Labor Party and the German SPD, but including all those who, like themselves, had moved verbally sharply leftward in response to mass discontent.

In short, they wanted a centrist international. So did the leaders of the German USPD, which was rapidly gaining ground at the expense of the SPD. The Swedish left social democrats, the Czechoslovak left wing, and smaller parties in other countries (including the British ILP) had essentially the same line. But pressure from their ranks forced them to pay lip service to the October Revolution and to negotiate for admission to the Communist International.

"The desire of certain leading 'center' groups to join the Third International," wrote Lenin, "provides indirect confirmation that it has won the sympathy of the vast majority of class-conscious workers throughout the world, and is becoming a more powerful force with each day."[1] But these parties were not revolutionary communist organizations. Their traditions were those of prewar social democracy—revolutionary in words, passive in practice. And they were led by men who would try any twist or turn in order to keep control and prevent the adoption of genuine revolutionary strategy and tactics.

Without the bulk of the members of these parties, the new International could not hope to exert a decisive influence in Europe in the short term. Without breaking with their centrist leaders, it could not hope to exert a *revolutionary* influence. Nor was the situation much different with the mass parties already inside the Comintern. The PSI, for example, had centrists and even some thoroughgoing reformists in its leadership.

The struggle against centrism was complicated by another factor. Strong ultraleftist currents—which wanted to reject *all* participation in bourgeois democratic institutions—existed inside many of the communist organizations. And outside them were some important syndicalist trade union organizations that rejected the workers' party as the instrument for achieving the overthrow of capitalism, looking instead to the mass organization of workers in trade unions. These had moved close to the Third International but still rejected the need for communist parties.

The Spanish syndicalist federation, the CNT, which had about a million members at the time, had voted for affiliation in December 1919. A strong minority of the French trade union federation, the CGT, was also in favor. Other syndicalist groups, such as the American Industrial Workers of the World (IWW), were undoubtedly revolutionary and were thought to be winnable. To gain and integrate these big forces was a difficult and complex operation. It required a struggle on several different fronts.

At the Second World Congress of the Comintern (July–August 1920), 217 delegates from sixty-seven organizations in some forty countries debated these various issues. Centrists and ultralefts were well represented. Both the SFIO and the USPD had delegations, but these were not permitted to vote. The decisions of the congress were of fundamental importance. In an important sense, this was the real founding congress. It took place at the height of the war between revolutionary Russia and Poland, when the Red Army was nearing Warsaw. In Germany, a right-wing attempt to establish a military dictatorship, the Kapp Putsch, had just been defeated by mass working-class action. In Italy, the factory occupations were about to begin. The mood of revolutionary optimism was stronger than ever.

Zinoviev, president of the International, declared: "I am deeply convinced that the Second World Congress of the Communist International is the precursor of another world congress, the world congress of Soviet Republics."[2] All that was needed were real mass communist parties to lead the movement to victory.

The twenty-one conditions

"Just as it is not easy for a camel to pass through the eye of a needle so, I hope, it will not be easy for the adherents of the center to slip through the twenty-one conditions. They are put forward to make clear to the workers in the USPD and in the Italian and French Socialist Parties, and to all organized workers, what the international general staff of the proletarian revolution demands of them."

Zinoviev, Speech at the Second World Congress

THE SECOND International had been a loose federation of national parties. The Third International was to be a centralized world party with national sections, although the International must take into account "the varying conditions in which the individual parties have to fight and work and…must take decisions of general validity only when such decisions are possible."[3] The various national programs were to be based on the International's program and subject to international approval. All decisions, not only those of congresses but also those of the Comintern executive between congresses, were to be binding on all the parties. This was the substance of the fifteenth and sixteenth of the twenty-one conditions for affiliation to the Third International put forward by the executive.

In light of later events, many critics have seen in these conditions the seeds of degeneration. They were put forward, it is argued, solely to ensure Russian dominance, to enable the Russians to manipulate the international movement in their own interests. The centrist critics of the conditions did not argue this case at the second congress. The reasons for this are obvious. After the experience of the 1914–18 war no one addressing an audience of revolutionaries could defend the methods and practices of the Second International. Everyone, apart from the syndicalists, paid at least lip service to the ideals of international unity and a world party.

Moreover everyone, not least the Russians themselves, expected that the exceptional position of the Russian party, as the only one in power, would be a strictly temporary affair. Lenin had written shortly before the congress: "Soon after the victory of the proletarian revolution in at least one of the advanced countries, a sharp change will probably come about: Russia will cease to be the model and will once again become a backward country (in the "soviet" and socialist sense)."[4]

The conditions that the USPD delegates, in particular, most objected to were the ones requiring "a complete and absolute break with reformism and with the policy of the center,"[5] and the expulsion of a number of named "notorious opportunists," including Kautsky and Rudolf Hilferding of the USPD, Filippo Turati and Giuseppe Modigliani of the (affiliated) PSI, Jean Longuet of the SFIO and Ramsay MacDonald, a future British prime minister, of the ILP. "They overlooked entirely," argued

Arthur Crispien for the USPD, "that we have separated from the Right Socialists, that we did not shrink from this break as soon as it became historically inevitable. Just the same this break should not be treated slightingly. I admit that a separation was a necessity.... The workers can be split much easier than they can be won and kept together for the revolution in Germany."[6] No more splits could be countenanced, he said.

The centrist leaders were prepared to make very radical noises. "We took a definite stand at the party conference in March," said Crispien, "and already then put into our program the dictatorship of the proletariat in unmistakable terms...we pointed out that parliamentarianism is not going to achieve socialism."[7]

The USPD would not, however, accept the twenty-one conditions, because that would mean a split with its own right wing. That at the beginning of 1919 the USPD had collaborated with the SPD to establish the Weimar Republic; that without this collaboration the operation would have been much more difficult if not impossible; that the revolutionism of most of the USPD leaders was purely verbal: All these things were carefully glossed over.

The USPD was of course a very heterogeneous party. Even in its leadership there were some whose subjective political ideas were revolutionary. But that leadership has to be judged not by words, or even good intentions, but by its deeds in the crucial months of November and December 1918.

On November 10, 1918, three thousand delegates of the Berlin workers' and soldiers' councils appointed as provisional government of Germany a Council of People's Commissars. They were Ebert, Scheidemann, and Landsberg of the SPD and Barth, Dittmann, and Haase of the USPD. There was no other government. The last chancellor of imperial Germany, Prince Max von Baden, had dissolved his government on November 9 and appointed Ebert as his successor. On the evening of the 10th, General Groener, the new chief of staff of the army, telephoned Ebert, "placing the army at the disposal of the new government."

All these actions, von Baden's and Groener's no less than those of the Berlin delegates, were entirely illegal. There was a revolution. The old regime had collapsed. Von Baden saw no hope for the German bourgeoisie except the SPD. Groener saw no hope of holding the army together except through the SPD. Actually, and this is centrally important, the army disintegrated nonetheless. After the signing of the armistice with the Western allies on November 11, the German general staff moved the entire western group of armies, two million soldiers, back across the Rhine. Once across the river, in Groener's own words, "the units simply melted away." The core of the state machine dissolved.

Now the SPD leaders, from the start, set out to reconstitute that state machine. Their two key decisions were the convening of a national assembly and the creation of a small new volunteer army under right-wing officers, which was then used against the revolutionary left in January 1919. The USPD leaders—half the government—supported the first move, and, although they were opposed to the second, they did not fight it.

These were the centrist leaders that the twenty-one conditions were designed to exclude. It is crystal clear that, given their recent record, no verbal commitment to workers' power or anything else by these leaders was of the slightest value. A split was absolutely necessary. Fortunately two of the three USPD leaders at the second congress, Crispien and Dittmann, opposed it openly—thereby facilitating a sharp debate.

The French centrists adopted a different tactic. Their main spokesman was the notorious opportunist Marcel Cachin. Cachin had not only been violently in favor of the First World War until 1917 but had acted as an agent of the French government in an attempt to create a pro-war wing in the Italian Socialist Party and had cooperated for this purpose with the renegade (and future fascist dictator) Benito Mussolini. Cachin was willing to promise anything. "We are in full agreement.... We are convinced that if our friend Longuet had been able to be here, his opinion, after consideration, would not have been different from ours [Longuet was an outspoken opponent of the Bolsheviks]. We shall return to France carrying your conditions."[8]

A party led by Longuet, Cachin, Ludovic Frossard, and their friends would never be a revolutionary party, whatever promises it made. Clearly, it was not going to be as easy as Zinoviev had supposed to prevent the centrist camels slipping through the needle's eye. For this reason, a number of left-wing delegates sharply criticized the executive of the Comintern for allowing the centrists to be present at all. Lenin disagreed. "When Kautsky attacks us and brings out books against us," he said, "we polemicize with him as our class enemy. But when the USPD, which has expanded as a result of an influx of revolutionary workers, comes here for negotiations, we must talk to its representatives, since they are a section of the revolutionary workers."[9]

After the congress, these workers could be reached more easily. After an intense debate in their party, the USPD leaders were compelled to call a congress at Halle, in October, to consider affiliation to the Comintern. The left won by 236 votes to 156. The right split. The new party, after uniting with the original German Communist Party (KPD), which had formed in 1919, counted some 350,000 members. The Comintern now had a mass party in the most important country in Europe. In December, the Tours congress of the French SFIO voted by a three-to-one majority (3,208 votes to 1,022) to affiliate and accept the twenty-one conditions. The resulting new French Communist Party (PCF) started with 150,000 members. But though the more uncompromising right-wingers, led by Longuet and Leon Blum, had split away to reestablish the SFIO, the PCF itself was led by "reconstructed" centrists such as Frossard and Cachin. Events were to prove that the reconstruction was only skin deep.

That same December 1920, the Czechoslovak Social Democratic Party split, the communist left taking over half the membership and establishing a communist party one hundred thousand strong. A separate split in the social democratic party of the German-speaking minority in Czechoslovakia (Sudetenland) added further forces, and, after the unification of these, the party claimed 170,000 members.

By early 1921, parties affiliated to the Comintern had the support of the majority of politically conscious European workers in six countries (France, Italy, Norway, Bulgaria, Yugoslavia, and Czechoslovakia) and of a substantial minority in others (Germany, Sweden, and Poland). The most important exception was Britain, where the Communist Party, founded in 1920, had perhaps three thousand real members (although claiming ten thousand) and was not yet a serious force.

It is useful at this point to look at some others of the twenty-one conditions. "The entire party press must be run by reliable communists...." stated one of these. "The periodical press and other publications, and all party publishing houses must be completely subordinated to the party, regardless of whether the party as a whole is at a given moment legal or illegal. Publishing houses must not be allowed to abuse their independence and pursue a policy which is not wholly in accordance with the policy of the party." This condition was aimed at the notorious way in which, in many social democratic parties, individuals with money or wealthy supporters ran allegedly party publications that were not under party control and that commonly accommodated to petty-bourgeois prejudices.

Another condition declared "no confidence in bourgeois legality:" "Where...communists are unable to do all their work legally, it is absolutely essential to combine legal and illegal work."

Again,

> Every party which wishes to join the Communist International is obliged to expose not only avowed social-patriotism, but also the insincerity and hypocrisy of social-pacifism; to bring home to the workers systematically that without the revolutionary overthrow of capitalism no international court of arbitration, no agreement to limit armaments, no 'democratic' reorganization of the League of Nations will be able to prevent new imperialist wars. [The modern equivalent of the League of Nations is the United Nations.]
>
> Every party...must carry on systematic and persistent communist activity inside the trade unions, the workers' councils and factory committees, the cooperatives and other mass workers' organizations. Within these organizations communist cells must be organized which shall by persistent and unflagging work win the trade unions, etc., for the communist cause.

This was, of course, directed against ultralefts in the communist parties—but it is worth noting that the problem of labor bureaucracies, as a conservative layer inside the mass workers' organizations, is not specifically considered.

> Parties belonging to the Communist International must be based on the principle of *democratic centralism*...the Communist Party will be able to fulfill its duty only if its organization is as centralized as possible, if iron discipline prevails, and if the party center, upheld by the confidence of the party mem-

bership, has strength and authority and is equipped with the most comprehensive powers.

The key phrase here is "upheld by the confidence of the party membership," for discipline in a revolutionary party is 90 percent a matter of conviction. The clause was aimed, first of all, against members of parliament, councilors, trade union officials, and other relatively privileged people within the party. An organization that does not force these to submit to the discipline of the party—or expel them when they do otherwise— is not a revolutionary socialist organization.

Naturally the emphasis, on democracy at one time, on centralism at another, depends on the requirements of the situation. Who decides what these requirements are? There can be no simple reliance on an "infallible" leadership, for there is no such thing. It is a matter of developing a layer of experienced members within the party—"cadre"—who are able to judge. But this takes time—something that the Comintern parties had precious little of in the crucial early years.

Other points in the twenty-one conditions dealt with party work in the armed forces, among the peasantry, in relation to colonies, and with international trade union affiliations, which will be considered later.

In practice, the new mass communist parties did not yet even approximate the model set out by the twenty-one conditions. They had all kinds of defects. But their very existence was an enormous step forward.

In the summer of 1920, still further forces, the big syndicalist organizations of France and Spain and smaller ones elsewhere, seemed open to influence. The problem was to convince them of the need for a revolutionary party. An important debate at the Second World Congress was on the nature of the revolutionary party and the syndicalist objections.

The role of the party

"The Communist International decisively rejects the view that the proletariat can achieve its revolution without having an independent political party of its own. Every class struggle is a political struggle. The goal of this struggle, which is inevitably transformed into civil war, is the conquest of political power.

Political power cannot be seized, organized, and operated, except through a political party."
                    Resolution of the Second World Congress

"IT MAY seem fairly strange that, three-quarters of a century after the appearance of *The Communist Manifesto*, discussion should arise at an international communist congress over whether a party is necessary or not," wrote Trotsky. In fact, he continued, the events of recent years "compel us to pose the question whether the party is necessary or not."[10]

The revolutionary syndicalists identified political parties with parliamentarianism—and identified participation in parliaments with opportunism and betrayal. Their alternative was militant trade unionism, based on direct action and leading ultimately to the revolutionary general strike. Parties were not only unnecessary, according to this viewpoint, they were a positive handicap to the working class. The betrayal of 1914 proved it.

"What matters most is that the spirit should be revolutionary...." said Pestana, delegate of the Spanish CNT. "The important thing is that the trade unions as such should be revolutionary and militant organizations."[11]

Jack Tanner, a future president of the British engineering workers' union, but speaking at the Congress for the British Shop Stewards and Workers' Committee Movement, developed the argument.

> Most of the active men in the shop stewards' movement have been members of the political socialist parties but have left them because they considered they were not traveling along the right path.... There is no question of returning like repentant sinners to the fold.... Now efforts are being made again to get the workers to resort to parliament, although all are agreed that it must be abolished as soon as possible. The English workers are losing faith in parliamentary action.... You will get nothing but antagonism from the class-conscious workers on the question of affiliation to the Labour Party.[12]

The Russian leaders badly wanted to win over the syndicalists as a revolutionary counterweight to the centrist waverers who were slipping into the Comintern. "Just because I know that the party is indispensable...and just because I see Scheidemann (leader of the German SPD) on the one side and, on the other, American or Spanish or French syndicalists who not only wish to fight against the bourgeoisie but who, unlike Scheidemann, really want to tear its head off," Trotsky declared, "I prefer to discuss with these Spanish, American and French comrades...to prove to them in a friendly way...and not by counterposing to them Scheidemann's long experience and saying that for the majority this question has already been settled."[13]

Zinoviev stressed the contrast between a social-democratic and a communist party.

> We need no parties which are actuated by the simple principle of getting into their ranks the greatest possible numbers of members, parties which degenerate into petty-bourgeois parties.... We want no such parties in which, for example, during election campaigns candidates are put up who only yesterday joined the party. We want no such parliamentary representation in which there are forty-six professors and forty-five lawyers or more.... It is understandable why there are good working men who say, "It is better to have no party at all than to have such a party."[14]

Bukharin, at the same congress, claimed that "of the sixty-eight socialist deputies in the French Chamber, forty were reformists, twenty-six centrists and only two communists.... Of the nineteen socialists in the Norwegian Storting [parliament], only two were communists."[15]

The communist organization proposed by the Comintern, Zinoviev emphasized, was totally different.

> The members of our party must be the best men in every industry. They will be a minority at first; but since they have a clearly defined program, since they are the best men, since they are known among the working people, they will, when the right hour comes, become immediately the leaders of the masses. The struggle that is coming is a gigantic one....
>
> Not shapeless labor unions which live from hand to mouth, but the party is what we need most, the party which comprises the best elements of the working class, who have been organized for years, who have formed the nucleus and who will point out to the working class the right road. The task is to organize the advance guard of the working class who will really be in a position to lead the masses in this struggle. In this fight, we cannot do without a general staff; we must create it, meaning that we must organize at once the best elements of the working class.[16]

The essence of the matter was summed up in the "theses" on the party question that were adopted at the congress.

A sharp distinction must be made between the concepts of party and class. The members of the Christian and Liberal trade unions of Germany, England, and other countries are undoubtedly part of the working class. The more or less numerous groups of workers who still follow Scheidemann, Samuel Gompers [head of the American Federation of Labor] and their like are undoubtedly part of the working class. In certain historical circumstances, it is even possible for the working class to include very numerous reactionary elements. It is the task of communism not to adapt itself to these backward sections...but to raise the entire working class to the level of the communist vanguard....

The revolutionary syndicalists often speak of the great part that can be played by a determined revolutionary minority. A really determined minority of the working class, a minority that is communist, that wants to act, that has a program, that is out to organize the struggle of the masses—that is precisely what the communist party is.[17]

A number of important syndicalist leaders, notably the Frenchmen Monatte and Rosmer, were won over. But clearly the affiliation of syndicalist trade union bodies, as such, was not a real possibility. It was partly to meet this difficulty that the Red International of Labor Unions was set up later.

"No compromise, no maneuvers"

"It would be absurd to formulate a recipe or general rule ('No Compromises!') to suit all cases. One must use one's own brains and be able to find one's bearings in each particular instance. It is, in fact, one of the functions of a party organization and of party leaders worthy of the name, to acquire, through the prolonged, persistent, variegated, and comprehensive efforts of all thinking representatives of a given class, the knowledge, experience and—in addition to knowledge and experience—the political flair necessary for the speedy and correct solution of complex political problems."

Lenin, *"Left-Wing" Communism, an Infantile Disorder*

IN LATE December 1918, the national congress of German workers' and soldiers' councils had voted by 344 to 98 to allow the election of a national assembly. The SPD leaders who pressed this line, which in effect meant the suicide of the workers' councils, undoubtedly enjoyed the support of a large majority of the working class at that moment. Almost immediately afterward the German Communist Party (KPD) held its founding congress. It voted by a big majority (62 to 23) to boycott the election. In this debate, those who had joined the KPD from the leadership of the old Spartakus League were almost unanimously in favor of participation. Rosa Luxemburg argued: "We wish to be prepared for all possibilities, including utilizing the National Assembly for revolutionary purposes, should the Assembly ever come into being."[18]

It was of course possible, in the circumstances, to make out a case of sorts for the boycott. It could have been argued that the workers' and soldiers' councils were still in existence and could be maintained; that the SPD was rapidly losing ground; that its majority in the councils could be quickly overturned; that an insurrection with mass support against the SPD-USPD government was possible in the near future. Such a case would have been based on a misreading of the situation, but it would not have been absurd.

This was *not* the case argued by most of those who advocated boycotting the election. For them, such calculations were irrelevant. They were for workers' councils and against parliaments. Therefore they must have nothing to do with any parliament. To do so could only confuse the workers: "All reversion to parliamentary forms of struggle...have become politically and historically obsolete," a group of the boycottists wrote a little later, "and any policy of maneuvering and compromise must be emphatically rejected."[19]

Politically obsolete for whom? In the National Assembly elections held on January 19, 1919, the SPD won eleven and a half million votes, overwhelmingly the votes of working men and women (this was the first German election held on the basis of universal suffrage). Parliamentarianism was certainly obsolete from the point of view of the few thousand members of the KPD and even, at that time, for a wider circle of working-class militants, perhaps some hundreds of thousands. But it was evidently not at all obsolete from the point of view of the millions of workers who voted for the SPD or the USPD.

The ultralefts assumed that what was clear to the advanced militant must also be clear to workers at large, and that those who did not accept it were either scoundrels who had been corrupted or sheep who were merely waiting for the correct lead to be given. These were the underlying assumptions of the young militants who had joined with the handful of old Spartakists to form the KPD. Such assumptions led to a policy of adventurism alternating with abstentionism.

On January 5, 1919, the still-tiny KPD, with the support of local sections of the USPD, attempted to seize power in Berlin. The rising, which later came to be known as the Spartakus rising, had not been planned in advance on the basis of a calculation of the balance of forces. It was the spontaneous reaction of KPD and some USPD militants to the attempt of the government to dismiss Emil Eichhorn, a left-wing USPD member who had taken over as chief of the Berlin police during the November 1918 revolution. The dismissal was a calculated provocation.

Luxemburg, Liebknecht, and the majority of the national leadership of the party were opposed to the rising. Liebknecht then changed his mind. The others were overruled and, reluctantly, put themselves at its head. The revolutionaries had some military support, notably that of about three thousand armed sailors from Kiel, but they were a definite minority in the still-existing Berlin council of workers' and soldiers' deputies.

Lacking majority working-class support, even in Berlin, the rising was soon crushed. Ebert, Scheidemann, and Gustav Noske, the SPD leaders, gave the cover of "socialist" and "republican" legality to hastily reconstructed right-wing army units led by former imperial officers. In the repression that followed, Rosa Luxemburg, Karl Liebknecht, and many others were murdered.

The KPD, or rather its local leadership in Munich, behaved better during the brief life of the Bavarian Soviet Republic that followed three months later (April 7 to May 1, 1919). It opposed the formation of the republic, correctly assessing it as an adventure resting on slender support, and only took over the leadership when the coalition of anarchists, USPD men, and some SPD supporters (which formed the "government") fell to pieces. The result of the defeat was that "Bavaria became the Land (province) with a perpetual state of emergency which hampered all attempts at socialist organization. The KPD went underground. Leaders not killed in the first days [of the counterrevolution] were sentenced by civil courts to long prison terms...."[20] The local KPD leaders could hardly be blamed for this outcome. They had done all they could have done. But they were not typical of the membership nationally. What Lenin called "the infantile disorder of ultraleftism" flourished. A majority of the party was not only opposed to participation in elections; it was equally opposed to working in the existing unions. "New forms of organization must be created...." declared the group previously quoted. "A Workers' Union, based on factory organizations, should be the rallying point for all revolutionary elements. This should unite all workers who follow the slogan 'Get out of the trade unions.' It is here that the militant proletariat musters its ranks for battle. Recognition of the class struggle, of the Soviet system and of the dictatorship should be sufficient for enrollment."[21]

Against this "old and familiar rubbish" Lenin had written, shortly before the 1920 congress of the Comintern, one of his most powerful polemics, titled *"Left-Wing" Communism*. At the congress itself a firm line was taken against abstentionism: "Communists in all countries must join the trade unions in order to turn them into conscious fighting organs for the overthrow of capitalism.... All voluntary abstention from the trade unions, all artificial attempts to create separate trade unions...are extremely dangerous for the communist movement."[22]

On the boycotting of parliaments, mindful of the struggle against centrism, the "theses" adopted by the congress carefully restated that,

> The form taken by the proletarian dictatorship is the Soviet Republic.... The task of the proletariat is to shatter the bourgeois state machine, to destroy it, and to destroy with it parliamentary institutions.... Consequently communism repudiates parliamentarianism as the form of the future society, as the form of the class dictatorship of the proletariat. It denies the possibility of winning parliament over permanently; its object is to destroy parliamentarianism.[23]

On the other hand,

> "Anti-parliamentarianism" on principle, that is, the absolute and categorical rejection of participation in elections and in revolutionary parliamentary activity, is...a naive and childish doctrine which is beneath contempt, a doctrine which is...blind to the possibility of the revolutionary parliamentari-

anism.... The boycotting of elections or of parliament are permissible primarily when the conditions for the immediate transition to armed struggle for power are at hand.[24]

Opposition to these views was by no means confined to Germany. The biggest section of the left of the PSI in Italy was strongly "boycottist in principle." A good proportion of the membership of the British, U.S., Dutch, and other communist parties was ultraleft. Thus the Dutch majority favored an "elite" organization of politically educated and sophisticated members, carefully selected, "undiluted" by raw militant workers, essentially propagandistic in practice, and very far from the "best representatives of the working class" approach of the Comintern. Its abstentionist attitude, expressed most clearly at the third congress of the Comintern in 1921, flowed from this.

By contrast, the U.S. Communist Party was ultra-revolutionary. A majority of its members were in favor of "underground and secret operations *only*." All attempts at open and "legal" activity were denounced as "opportunism." The British Communist Party, although never committed to either of these absurdities, nevertheless had a strong ultraleft streak in its first year or two. In fact, ultraleftism, both of the abstentionist and adventurist variants, was strong in the early years of the Comintern and was to reassert itself powerfully in 1924–25 as well as, under different circumstances, in 1928–34, as we shall see.

Where it mattered most, in Germany, the ultraleft wing had been excluded from the KPD at the party's second congress, which was held, illegally, in Heidelberg in October 1919. The surviving Spartakist leaders—Levi, Meyer, and others—had forced through resolutions making acceptance of trade union work and rejection of election boycotts "on principle" a condition of membership. It was done with scant regard for democratic procedures (some of the "left" delegates were not told the time and place of the meeting) and it cost the party half or more of its growing membership.[25] But it was essential if the KPD was ever to become a real force and, in particular, it was a necessary condition for the fusion with the left wing of the USPD that was achieved a year later.

The "lefts" later formed the Communist Workers' Party (KAPD), which claimed, initially, thirty-eight thousand members but which fell to pieces in the next few years. It was allowed a nonvoting delegation at the Second World Congress of the Comintern.

Yet, even after the exclusion of the "lefts," the KPD was far from having acquired the "political flair" of which Lenin had written. On March 13, 1920, a section of the reconstituted German Army under General Lüttwitz, the conqueror of the Spartakus rising, turned and bit the hand that fed it. It seized Berlin and deposed the Social Democratic government of the Weimar Republic, appointed by the National Assembly. Ebert and his colleagues fled to Stuttgart. The rest of the army stayed "neutral": it would not fight for the Weimar Republic. This was the Kapp Putsch, so called after a civilian reactionary, Dr. Kapp, who acted as Lüttwitz's frontman.

The German trade union federation called an unlimited general strike. More than twelve million workers came out. Armed resistance to the putsch developed, especially in the Ruhr and in Saxony, led by individuals and groups of members of the USPD and of both communist parties. Yet the first reaction of the KPD center was to declare its neutrality in a fight between "two counterrevolutionary gangs"!

"The proletariat will not lift a finger for the democratic republic,"[26] it stated. This staggering failure to realize what was at stake, the assumption that there is no difference between a military dictatorship and a bourgeois-democratic republic, indicates the extent to which ultraleftism had affected even its declared opponents.

This abstentionist stand was quickly reversed. Fortunately most of the party members were in advance of their leaders and ignored it from the beginning. The Kapp Putsch collapsed after a few days of intense and increasingly violent working-class resistance. The result was a marked swing to the left amongst German workers. The USPD gained five million votes in the subsequent election and the KPD, which became a legal organization after the defeat of the putsch, half a million.

> The Kapp Putsch was decisive in the development of German Communism. Until this time, the Spartakists had been an isolated minority.... The Kapp Putsch stimulated new impulses in the USPD. After a two-year experience with Lüttwitz, von Seeckt, von Walter, Eberhardt, the workers were convinced that these men would not be disarmed by well-rounded formulas: they had lost their hope that the Social Democratic gov-

ernment would act against the open and secret rearmament of the restoration.[27]

The members of the KPD and USPD grew closer together. The basis for the victory at Halle had been laid in united action between them. But a strong streak of ultraleftism survived in the new mass united communist party (VKPD) that resulted from their fusion, as the "March Action" of 1921 was to prove. An experienced cadre, such as the Bolsheviks had in Russia, could not easily be improvised.[28]

The British Communist Party and the British Labor Party

"It should be borne in mind that the British Labor Party is in a very special position: it is a highly original type of party, or rather, it is not at all a party in the ordinary sense of the word. It is made up of members of all trade unions, and has a membership of about four million, and allows sufficient freedom to all affiliated political parties. It thus includes a vast number of British workers who follow the lead of the worst bourgeois elements, who are even worse than Scheidemann, Noske, and similar people. At the same time, however, the Labor Party has let the British Socialist Party into its ranks, permitting it to have its own press organs in which members of the self-same Labor Party can freely and openly declare that the party leaders are social traitors.... This is a very original situation: a party which unites enormous masses of workers, so that it might seem a political party, is nevertheless obliged to grant its members complete latitude.... In such circumstances, it would be a mistake not to join the party."
Lenin, Speech at the Second World Congress

THE MAIN characteristics of the British Communist Party (CPGB), formed at the end of July 1920, were its extreme weakness and its political inheritance—the sectarian, propagandist traditions of British Marxism.

Its main forces came from the British Socialist Party, the lineal descendant of H. M. Hyndman's Social Democratic Federation (later the Social Democratic Party and then, from 1912, the British Socialist Party). Engels had regarded the SDF as hopelessly sectarian, passive, and propagandistic. The SDF-SDP-BSP had always been a sect, although at times a fairly large sect. Other forces had joined the Communist Party from the Socialist Labor Party, a breakaway from the SDF, still sectarian but a much more activist and interventionist group; from the remnants of the wartime shop stewards' movement, and from a few other sources. The new party had, nevertheless, only about three thousand members altogether, and many of these were to drop out in the next couple of years.

This weakness was not, of course, merely an accident of personalities or ideas. In the last resort, it was the product of the overwhelming dominance of British capitalism throughout most of the nineteenth century. After the historic defeats of the British working class in the first half of the century, this had shaped the working-class movement along very narrow, sectionalist, and "subordinate" lines.

For these reasons, there had been no mass social democratic party in Britain before 1914. Now this was changing. The Labor Party, which had been a small and very moderate parliamentary pressure group closely allied to the dominant Liberal Party, declared itself a socialist organization in 1918 and began to set up local branches open to individual members. In the general election of that year, it fought independently of—and against—the Liberals for the first time and, profiting from the radicalization produced by the First World War, gained 22 percent of the total vote. It was still very much a federal body ("not at all a party in the ordinary sense of the word"), and the British Socialist Party was one of its affiliated constituents. Of course this state of affairs could not be expected to last long but, in 1920, the situation was still to some degree fluid.

The Comintern executive, and Lenin in particular, urged the British Communist Party to intervene in the Labor Party by affiliating to it and carrying on a fight for revolutionary politics inside its ranks. Although Lenin called the Labor Party "a thoroughly bourgeois party, because, although made up of workers, it is led by reactionaries, and the worst kind of reactionaries at that,"[29] he argued: "If the British Communist Party starts by acting in a revolutionary manner in the Labor Party, and if the Hendersons [he was Labor Party general secretary] are obliged to expel this party, that will be a great victory for the communist and revolutionary working-class movement in Britain."[30]

The idea was to wrench the British Communist Party away from its propagandist heritage, to win layers of the newly awakened workers away from the Hendersons and MacDonalds of the Labor Party, and so lay the basis for an *interventionist* communist party of some size and substance. The twelve British delegates at the congress were divided on the issue, but, back in Britain, the British Communist Party's founding conference had voted by 100 votes to 85 to apply for affiliation to the Labor Party a few days before Lenin's speech on the question.

The application for affiliation in August 1920 was rejected by the Labor Party executive, but the Communist Party persisted. "Our tactic then," wrote party leader Tom Bell, "was not to accept a refusal by the Labor Party but to carry the campaign into the country, that is, to go to the local Labor Parties, to the trade union branches...we were met by a variety of circumstances. Some local Labor Parties, dominated by the reactionary elements who found the communists troublesome, naturally took the opportunity to follow the lead of Henderson and the Labor Party executive, to exclude the communists from the local Labor Parties. In other localities, where the communists had already been working well and had influence in trade union organizations and the local workers' movement, the local parties were inclined to be sympathetic and not to take any action against the communists. The whole content of this campaign raised the question of soviets versus the parliamentary democracy and brought to the front the question of the role of violence in the struggle for power."[31]

Undoubtedly it was a fruitful operation in the circumstances, especially in terms of orienting the new Communist Party on the mass movement. If the gains were less than had been hoped for, this was, above all, due to the sharp downturn of the class struggle in Britain following the betrayal of the miners by the Triple Alliance of trade unions and their subsequent defeat by the employers in 1921. That, and the wage cuts successfully imposed on the engineering workers, shipyard workers, seamen, cotton-trade operatives, and printers, naturally strengthened the right wing in the unions and so, inevitably, strengthened the right wing in the Labor Party against the Communist Party.

Nevertheless, the affiliation campaign, at least in its first years, laid the basis for the subsequent application of the united front tactic around the National Minority Movement in the unions. Of course, the Communist Party's attempt to affiliate to the Labor Party was not an "entry" operation, as that term later came to be understood. There was never any question of the British Communist Party giving up either political or organizational independence. It remained an open revolutionary party. The campaign was an example of the combination of firm, principled political positions with a great tactical flexibility, a characteristic of the Comintern leadership in these early years, though not, unfortunately, of the Comintern parties as a whole.

The peasants and the colonial world

"The question was posed as follows: are we to consider as correct the assertion that the capitalist stage of economic development is inevitable for backward nations...? We replied in the negative. If the victorious revolutionary proletariat conducts systematic propaganda amongst them, and the soviet governments come to their aid with all the means at their disposal—in that event it will be mistaken to assert that the backward peoples must inevitably go through the capitalist stage of development."
Lenin, Speech at the Second World Congress

IN 1847, Marx had predicted the development of large-scale industry, the growth of a large modern working class, and the destruction of the older classes in society: the independent craftsmen, peasants, and petty producers. The prediction had been brilliantly vindicated, but the process was an uneven one. Essentially, in 1920, large-scale industry was still confined to Europe and North America, apart from a few enclaves in the rest of the world. For the majority of the world's population, primitive forms of production were still the norm.

Even in Europe, uneven development was marked, above all in agriculture, where the process of capitalist concentration was very slow. Apart from Britain (or more exactly England and Lowland Scotland), numerically large peasantries survived in every European country, including such advanced countries as

France and Germany. No doubt, in the long run, peasant agriculture was doomed. Meanwhile, a perspective of revolution in the near future required a policy to win the mass of the peasants.

In Russia, where the peasants were a large majority of the population, the Bolsheviks had, as Lenin wrote, "entered into an informal (and very successful) political bloc with the petty-bourgeois peasantry by adopting the Socialist Revolutionary agrarian program in its entirety, without a single alteration."[32] The Socialist Revolutionary Party was the main peasant party during 1917 and the substance of its agrarian program was "the land to the peasants."

Many European communists were uneasy about this policy. They pointed to the undeniable fact that a landowning peasantry was an obstacle to the development of socialism. They failed to see that peasant support was essential to the overthrow of capitalism.

The centrists took the same line. At the Second World Congress, Crispien of the USPD accused the Russians of opportunism on the agrarian question. Serrati, leader of the center group in the PSI, took a wholly negative view of peasant movements. "Everyone knows that the movement for the occupation of lands—which was carried out, especially in Sicily, by veterans and Populari [a Catholic party with substantial peasant support]—was a demagogic and petty-bourgeois movement."[33] Therefore, turn one's back on it! This was in a country with a massive peasantry.

Crispien was also speaking after the disastrous experience of the Hungarian Soviet Republic. Hungary in 1919 was a country in which the peasant majority of the people lived on the estates of great landowners under near-feudal conditions. The Soviet Republic was established peacefully on March 21. The old regime had collapsed under the impact of military defeat, mass strikes, army mutiny, and the insistence of France and Britain on the cession of territories, which meant that 30 percent of all Magyar (Hungarian) speakers were to be transferred to the Anglo-French client states of Romania, Czechoslovakia, and Yugoslavia.

The Hungarian Soviet Government included the social democrats, who played a vacillating and treacherous role, as well as the communists, and it enjoyed the support of practically the whole working class. A Red Army was hastily organized. "The soviet government nationalized industry and the banks, introduced an eight-hour working day, disestablished the church (the biggest single landowner), introduced free school tuition and handed over palaces, villas, and sanatoriums for the use of the working people."[34]

What it did not do was to give the mass of the Magyar people, the peasants, a stake in the new order. In spite of advice and entreaties from Moscow, the great estates were simply nationalized and "the establishment of the proletarian dictatorship hardly changed anything in the Hungarian countryside, the day laborers saw no changes, and the small peasants got nothing."[35]

Romanian and Czechoslovak armies, directed by French officers, invaded Hungary. The Red Republic held out with desperate determination for 133 days, until August 1. After its fall, a white terror practically destroyed the workers' movement. The great magnates recovered their estates.

The soviet government, headed by Béla Kun, had made a number of avoidable errors but the one great error that was decisive was the doctrinaire refusal to compromise, to make serious concessions to the peasants. As a result, some three Hungarians out of four had, as they saw it, nothing to lose by the defeat of the working class. The Second World Congress declared: "It is urgently necessary that the conditions of the rural masses, the most exploited of them, should be immediately and appreciably improved by the victory of the proletariat, at the expense of the exploiters, for without that, the industrial proletariat cannot rely confidently on support from the countryside or on the provisioning of the towns with food."[36]

These considerations were of still greater importance in the colonial world. By world standards, even Hungary was an advanced society. "The vast majority of the world's population, over a thousand million, perhaps even 1,250 million people, if we take the total population of the world at 1,750 million," Lenin declared in his report on the national and colonial questions, "in other words, about 70 percent of the world's population belong to the oppressed nations, which are either in a state of direct colonial dependence or are semi-colonies, as, for example, Persia, Turkey, and China.... It would be utopian to believe that proletarian parties in these backward countries, if indeed they can emerge in them, can pursue communist tactics and a communist policy, without establishing definite relations with the peasant movement and without giving it effective support."[37]

But what, in any case, was the perspective for these countries? The material basis of socialism, a developed industry and a high productivity of labor, hardly existed there. The necessary human basis of socialism, a modern working class, was weak or even absent. Must they then follow the path taken by the advanced countries, the path of capitalist development?

Lenin's answer, endorsed by the Second World Congress, was a conditional negative. If the working class gained power in a number of advanced countries, if it came to the aid of the backward ones "with all the means at…[its] disposal," then the capitalist road of development was not inevitable.

Nearly forty years earlier, Engels had written to Kautsky in a similar though less confident vein. "Once Europe is reorganized (i.e., socialist), and North America, that will furnish such colossal power and such an example that the semi-civilized countries will of themselves follow in their wake; economic needs, if anything, will see to that," but he cautiously added: "But as to what social and political phases these countries will then have to pass through before they likewise arrive at socialist organization, I think we today can advance only rather idle hypotheses."[38]

There was, nonetheless, a difference between Lenin's view in 1920 and Engels's view in 1882. For Engels, the role of the backward countries was essentially passive. For Lenin, they had an active part to play. The difference arose from Lenin's conception of the development of imperialism, especially the export of capital from advanced imperialist states to backward colonial and semi-colonial ones, leading to developed capitalist states becoming "the rentier state…a state of parasitic, decaying capitalism."[39] This meant that the "rentier capitalism" of Britain and France could be attacked in India and China as well as in Britain and France.

Therefore, "our policy must be to bring into being a close alliance of all national and colonial liberation movements with Soviet Russia."[40] The problems of the relations of communist parties in backward areas with these bourgeois national liberation movements were already a matter of some controversy in 1920.

Lenin, presenting the report of the commission on the national and colonial questions at the Second World Congress, said:

> I should like especially to emphasize the question of the bourgeois-democratic movement in backward countries. This is a question that has given rise to certain differences. We have discussed whether it would be right or wrong, in principle and in theory, to state that the Communist International and the communist parties must support the bourgeois-democratic movement in backward countries...we have arrived at the unanimous decision to speak of the national revolutionary movement rather than of the bourgeois-democratic movement.
>
> It is beyond doubt that any national movement can only be a bourgeois-democratic movement, since the overwhelming mass of the population in the backward countries consists of peasants who represent bourgeois-capitalist relations.... It would be utopian to believe that proletarian parties in these backward countries, if indeed they can emerge in them, can pursue communist tactics and a communist policy, without establishing definite relations with the peasant movement and without giving it effective support. However, the objections have been raised that, if we speak of the bourgeois-democratic movement, we shall be obliterating all distinctions between the reformist and revolutionary movements. Yet that distinction has been very clearly revealed of late in the backward and colonial countries.... There has been a certain rapprochement between the bourgeoisie of the exploiting countries and that of the colonies, so that very often—perhaps even in most cases— the bourgeoisie of the oppressed countries, while it does support the national movement, is in full accord with the imperialist bourgeoisie, i.e., joins forces with it against all revolutionary movements and revolutionary classes...we, as communists, should and will support bourgeois liberation movements only when they are genuinely revolutionary and when their exponents do not hinder our work of educating and organizing in a revolutionary spirit the peasantry and the mass of the exploited.[41]

But the "bourgeois liberation movement" that does *not* fear the arousal of "the mass of the exploited" is not to be found in the twentieth century. What then? The Chinese Revolution of 1925–27 was decisively to expose the contradictions in this.

However, the actual "theses" adopted at the Second World Congress were unequivocal on the central practical question:

> A resolute struggle must be waged against the attempt to clothe the revolutionary liberation movements in the back-

ward countries which are not genuinely communist in communist colors. The Communist International has the duty of supporting the revolutionary movement in the colonies and backward countries only with the object of rallying the constituent elements of the future proletarian parties—which will be truly communist and not only in name—in all the backward countries, and educating them to a consciousness of their special task, namely, that of fighting against the bourgeois-democratic trend in their own nation.

The Communist International should collaborate *provisionally* with the revolutionary movement of the colonies and backward countries, and even form an alliance with it, but it must not amalgamate with it; it must *unconditionally maintain the independence of the proletarian movement*, even if it is only in an embryonic stage.[42] (Emphasis added.)

In pursuit of these policies, a "Congress of the Peoples of the East" was organized in Baku in September 1920. One thousand eight hundred and ninety-one "delegates" reportedly attended, the great majority of them Turks, Iranians, peoples of the Caucasus or of Russian Central Asia. The theme was "a modern crusade of oppressed people against the imperialist oppressors, with Britain as the main target of attack."[43] Although two-thirds of the "delegates" were said to be communists, most of them seem to have been from the territories of the old tsarist empire. The Turks, the biggest group from outside Russia, were for the most part simply nationalists opposed to the British and Greek intervention against Turkey. At that time, there was hardly a genuine communist party in Asia outside the lands held by the Red Army.

A subsequent "Congress of the Toilers of the Far East" (January–February 1922), although much smaller (144 delegates) was probably more significant. The delegations were real, representing actual organizations, and the Chinese, Koreans, and Mongols at least represented embryonic communist parties.

For the communist parties of the advanced countries, the line was clear and sharp. The eighth condition for affiliation to the Comintern required:

A particularly explicit and clear attitude on the question of the colonies.... Every party...is obliged to expose the tricks and dodges of "its" imperialists in the colonies, to support every colonial liberation movement, not merely in words but in deeds, to demand the expulsion of their own imperialists from these colonies…and to carry on systematic agitation among the troops of their country against any oppression of the colonial peoples.[44]

This was not only a decisive break with the "Eurocentrism" of the Second International but also a deepening of the gulf between reformist and revolutionary politics in the advanced countries.

Women and revolution

"The Third Congress of the Communist International declares that the tasks of the Communist Parties…include the following: to educate women in communist ideas and draw them into the ranks of the party; to fight the prejudices against women held by the mass of the male proletariat."

Methods and Forms of Work amongst Communist Party Women, Theses of the Third Congress of the Communist International (emphasis added)

IT IS a myth that the Comintern, in its period under Lenin, ignored the question of women's liberation. The subject was on the agenda of both the first and second congresses. Although the definitive "theses" were adopted at the third congress—by which time two international communist women's conferences had been held—it is convenient to consider them here.

First the analysis. The thesis stated:

[For] working women of the whole world…their liberation from centuries of enslavement, lack of rights and inequality is possible *only through the victory of communism*…the bourgeois women's movement is completely incapable of guaranteeing women that which communism gives.

So long as the power of capital and private property exists, the liberation of women from dependence on a husband can go no further than the right to dispose of her own property and her own wage and to decide on equal terms with her husband the future of her children…. The experience of working women in all those capitalist countries in which, over recent years, the bourgeoisie has introduced formal equality of the sexes makes this clear.

The vote does not destroy the prime cause of women's enslavement in the family and society. Some bourgeois states have substituted civil marriage for indissoluble marriage. But so long as the proletarian woman remains economically dependent on the capitalist boss and her husband, the breadwinner, and in the absence of comprehensive measures to protect motherhood and childhood and provide socialized child care and education, this cannot equalize the position of women in marriage or solve the problem of relationships between the sexes.

The real equality of women, as opposed to formal and superficial equality, will be achieved only under communism, when women and all other members of the working class will become co-owners of the means of production and distribution and will take part in administering them, and women will share on an equal footing with all members of the labor society the duty to work; in other words, it will be achieved by overthrowing the capitalist system of production and exploitation which is based on the exploitation of human labor, and by organizing a communist economy.[45]

Second, the solution in terms of struggle. Liberation will be won "not by the united efforts of women of different classes but by the united struggle of all the exploited...nor should there be a special women's movement and...any alliance between working women and bourgeois feminism, or support for the vacillating or clearly right-wing tactics of the social-compromisers and opportunists, will lead to a weakening of the forces of the working class, thereby delaying the great hour of the emancipation of women."[46]

The "united struggle of all the exploited" means participation in the class struggle. On these grounds, the Comintern rejected "a special women's movement." On the other hand, given the "prejudices against women held by the mass of the male proletariat," special measures were necessary by communist parties, *both* to fight male prejudice in their own ranks (as well as in the working class at large) *and* to draw women into active and leading roles in the parties themselves.

All this, in the early 1920s, when many social democrats could not yet agree that women should be allowed even to vote on the same terms as men, and when the bourgeois women's movements had supported the First World War!

The Comintern set up an elaborate structure of an international women's secretariat, international conferences, national women's secretariats, and so on. No doubt much of this remained on paper. But in the light of reformist—and worse—criticisms by feminists today, it can reasonably be said: This is our tradition; where were *your* political friends at the time?

THREE

THE EBB

"In the most critical year for the bourgeoisie, the year 1919, the proletariat of Europe could undoubtedly have conquered state power with minimum sacrifices, had there been at its head a genuine revolutionary organization, setting forth clear aims and capably pursuing them, i.e., a strong Communist Party. But there was none.... During the last three years, the workers have fought a great deal and have suffered many sacrifices. But they have not won power. As a result, the working masses have become more cautious than they were in 1919–20."

Trotsky, "The Main Lesson of the Third Congress," 1921

WHAT SHOULD a revolutionary party do in a nonrevolutionary situation? In 1919, this was not an issue. By 1921, it was central. As the Theses on the World Situation, adopted by the Third World Congress in 1921, put it:

> During the year that has passed between the second and third congresses of the Communist International, a series of working-class risings and struggles have ended in partial defeat [the advance of the Red Army on Warsaw in August 1920, the movement of the Italian proletariat in September 1920, the rising of the German workers in March 1921].
>
> The first period of the postwar revolutionary movement, distinguished by the spontaneous character of its assaults, by the marked imprecision of its aims and methods, and by the extreme panic which it aroused amongst the ruling classes, seems in essentials to be over. The self-confidence of the bourgeoisie as a class, and the outward stability of their state organs, have undeniably been strengthened.... The leaders of the bourgeoisie are even boasting of the power of their state machines and have

gone over to an offensive against the workers in all countries both on the economic and on the political front.[1]

A sober attempt to assess the actual situation, however unwelcome, and to relate to it, was the hallmark of the Comintern in Lenin's time—not revolutionary rhetoric.

The recovery of capitalism was shaky and uneven. 1921 saw the onset of a serious, if short-lived, economic crisis. Nevertheless, the receding of the revolutionary wave of 1919–20 meant that the immediate perspective of which Zinoviev had spoken in 1920, the World Congress of Soviet Republics, was now unreal. Revolutionary opportunities could, and indeed did, arise in the next few years. But the international movement as a whole had to come to terms with a new situation.

In Russia, the year 1921 saw the abandonment of "war communism" and the adoption of the "New Economic Policy" (NEP), a policy that Lenin described as "a strategical retreat." "We said, in effect," he wrote, "'Before we are completely routed, let us retreat and reorganize everything, but on a firmer basis.' If Communists deliberately examine the question of the New Economic Policy, there cannot be the slightest doubt that we have sustained a very severe defeat on the economic front."[2]

The NEP was, above all, a concession to the peasant majority of the population who, with the end of the civil war, was increasingly turning against the Soviet regime. Compulsory requisitioning of grain, which had fed the armies and the cities throughout the civil war, was abandoned and a fixed and moderate tax (in kind, for the currency had become worthless) substituted for it. Private trade and private small-scale production were legalized and encouraged. A new currency, based on gold, was introduced, and the test of profitability was applied by the state-owned banks in advancing and withholding credit to private and, with a few exceptions, public enterprises alike. Inevitably, unemployment reappeared in the cities—and it was fairly heavy throughout most of the rest of the decade—and petty capitalism flourished.

There was no alternative to these moves other than increasing repression against the peasant majority, and that, of course, would have destroyed the workers' state from within in a very short time, for the weakened, shrunken working class was itself heavily influenced by peasant discontent. The NEP was a holding operation, not a long-term solution to the problems of the beleaguered revolution. Such a solution depended on the workers of "one or more advanced countries," as Lenin wrote, taking and holding power. Meanwhile, it was necessary to change tack. On the international field, a corresponding turn was essential. This was not at all a question of an automatic reflection of events in Russia. The changed situation in the world outside Russia, above all in Europe, was one of the two main factors forcing the retreat to the NEP.

That changed situation put the choice squarely before European communists (and communism was still, in 1921, essentially a European movement): find ways and means of making revolutionary politics meaningful and important to workers in a (for the time being) nonrevolutionary situation, or face relegation to the position of revolutionary sects without serious influence on the course of events.

"From the day of its foundation," declared the Third World Congress's Theses on Tactics, "the Communist International has clearly and unambiguously made its goal the formation not of small communist sects, trying by propaganda and agitation only to establish their influence over the working masses, but participation in the struggle of the working masses, the direction of this struggle in a communist spirit, and the creation in the course of this struggle of experienced, large, revolutionary, mass communist parties."[3]

After stating that there was no permanent reformist solution to any of the problems facing the working class, after reaffirming that the destruction of capitalism remained the "guiding and immediate mission," the Theses argued:

> But to carry out this mission, the communist parties must put forward demands whose fulfillment is an immediate and urgent working class need, and they must fight for these demands in mass struggle, regardless of whether they are compatible with the profit economy of the capitalist class or not…. The task of the communist parties is to extend, to deepen, and to unify this struggle for concrete demands…. Every objection to the putting forward of such partial demands, every charge of reformism on this account, is an emanation of the same inability to grasp the essential conditions of revolutionary action as was expressed in the hostility of some revolutionary groups to participation in the trade unions or to

making use of parliament. It is not a question of proclaiming the final goal to the proletariat, but of intensifying the practical struggle, which is the only way of leading the proletariat to the struggle for the final goal.[4]

Powerful tendencies in a number of important communist parties rejected this approach. For them, the struggle for "partial and immediate demands" smacked of reformism. A set of ultraleftist amendments to the Theses on Tactics was submitted by the German, Austrian, and Italian parties.

Lenin wrote later: "At that [third] congress I was on the extreme right flank. I am convinced that it was the only correct stand to take."[5]

Ultraleftist ideas had gained sustenance in the course of the struggle against centrism, a struggle that was far from ended in 1921. Indeed, the two trends to some extent reinforced each other. This can be seen from the contrasting examples of Italy and Germany. The debacle into which the centrist leadership of the Italian party had led the working class in the autumn of 1920 encouraged the ultraleft adventurism of the "theory of the offensive" in Germany.

The Italian debacle

"The present phase of the class struggle in Italy is the phase that precedes either the conquest of political power by the revolutionary proletariat...or a tremendous reaction by the capitalists and the governing caste. Every kind of violence will be used to subjugate the agricultural and industrial working class."
Antonio Gramsci, writing in *L'Ordine Nuovo*, May 1920

ITALY EMERGED from the First World War as the weakest of the "victors." Its rulers had little to show for the half a million dead and the huge war debt. The cost of living had risen sixfold since before the war and was still climbing. The result was two years that have gone down in Italian history as the *Biennio Rosso*—the Two Red Years.

Workers in both town and country flooded into the trade unions. The socialist union federation, the CGL, had only 250,000 members at the end of the war. By the autumn of 1920, it had two million. Catholic and revolutionary syndicalist union federations also mushroomed. "During 1919 wave after wave of strikes, land occupations, demonstrations, street actions, conflict, broke over the country."[6] In June and July 1919, nationwide demonstrations over food prices reached insurrectionary proportions in a number of areas. There was a widely supported two-day national strike in solidarity with Soviet Russia. In the great industrial center of Turin, engineering workers began forming factory councils.

In the south and other agricultural areas, peasants, often led by ex-soldiers, occupied the land. And in the army itself, there were a number of mutinies. In the general election of November 1919, the Socialist Party (PSI), already affiliated to the Comintern, took nearly one-third of the votes.

The strike wave rolled on into 1920, reaching a new high point in April when half a million workers in the Turin region struck in defense of their factory councils. Only two months later, Serrati, leader of the centrist majority of the PSI (known as the "maximalists"), could declare to the Second World Congress of the Comintern: "Thus the political and economic conditions in Italy are such that they inevitably drive towards revolution. The party is so powerful that it may be said that the Italian proletariat is almost ready to seize power."[7]

The PSI, however, had no plan for any such thing. As we have seen, Serrati and the rest of the maximalist leadership of the PSI had refused to support the peasant land seizures on the grounds that they were "demagogic and petty-bourgeois." They had condemned the factory council movement in Turin as "the realm of aberration." The maximalists also tolerated within the ranks of the Socialist Party a minority of open reformists who were not only strong in the party's parliamentary group but also controlled the massive CGL union federation. In April, both the maximalists and the CGL leaders had stood by passively while the Turin workers struck in defense of their factory councils and went down to defeat.

The real test for the politics of the PSI leaders came in September 1920. From May onward, the metalworkers' section of the CGL had been pursuing their wage claim. Negotiations finally broke down in August and a special conference of the metalworkers' union decided on a slowdown. On August 30, one Milan employer locked out his workforce. Immediately

Milan metalworkers occupied all their factories in the city. On August 31, the engineering employers made the lockout nationwide—and by September 4, half a million metalworkers had occupied their factories throughout Italy.

This famous "occupation of the factories" was no ordinary wage dispute. Factory councils controlled the occupied plants. "Red guards" defended them. The occupying workers continued production, often supplied with deliveries by the railway workers union. In a number of cases the occupations were spread to neighboring gasworks and chemical plants.

The following story sums up the mood: The representative of a transport firm phoned the Fiat factory in Turin hoping to speak to the manager:

"Hello. Who's there?"

"This is the Fiat soviet."

"Ah!.... Pardon.... I'll ring again...."[8]

The mood owed much to the propaganda of the maximalist leadership of the PSI over the previous years. As Trotsky explained shortly afterward: "Everything written in *Avanti* [the party's daily paper] and everything uttered by the spokesmen of the Socialist Party was taken by the masses as a summons to the proletarian revolution. And this propaganda struck a responsive chord in the hearts of the working class, awakened their will and called forth the September events."

But, as Trotsky added; "The PSI verbally conducted a revolutionary policy, without ever taking into account any of its consequences. Everybody knows that during the September events no other organization so lost its head and became so paralyzed by fear as the PSI, which had itself paved the way for these events."[9]

There was no exaggeration in Trotsky's verdict. As revolutionary fervor mounted in the factories, the maximalist leaders of the PSI and the reformist leaders of the CGL (who, remember, were also PSI members) gathered in Milan. First, the union leaders questioned the representatives of the Turin workers. Would Turin kindly start the armed insurrection? Knowing that these same union leaders had left the Turin workers to fight alone in April, the Turin representatives of course said no.

The CGL leaders turned to the national directorate of the Socialist Party. "You believe this is the moment for revolution.

You assume the responsibility. We submit our resignation." The maximalists' bluff was called. They now backed off on the grounds that it was "too grave a responsibility."

Instead the question was put to the special congress of the CGL on September 11. There were two motions. One, from the CGL leaders, called for a struggle for "union control" of production (even the reformist union leaders now recognized that there was no possibility of ending the struggle on the basis of wages alone). The other motion, from the Socialist Party leaders, called for the movement to be put under their direction to be led "toward the maximum solution of the socialist program." Predictably, the union leaders' motion won—by 591,245 votes to 409,569. The maximalist leaders must have heaved a sigh of relief. At any rate, they were eager to stress that they were willing to abide by the "democratic decision."

By the end of the month, all the factories had been handed back to the employers in return for a wage increase and the setting up of a commission to draft legislation for "union control." For all its revolutionary rhetoric, the maximalist leadership of the PSI had failed absolutely to give any concrete lead to the hundreds of thousands of workers it influenced and the millions they influenced in turn. Instead it had engaged in a bureaucratic charade with the reformist union leaders in Milan.

The Comintern had endeavored to shift the maximalists from afar. Late in August, its executive had sent a letter to the PSI signed by Bukharin, Lenin, and Zinoviev:

> In Italy there are at hand all the most important conditions for a genuinely popular, great proletarian revolution.... Every day brings news of disturbances. All eyewitnesses—including the Italian delegates—assert and reiterate that the situation in Italy is profoundly revolutionary. Nevertheless, in many cases, the party stands aside, without attempting to generalize the movement, to give it slogans...to turn it into a decisive offensive against the bourgeois state.[10]

On September 22, when it was, as it turned out, already too late, the Comintern executive sent another urgent call to the party leaders.

> You cannot win by the seizure of factories and workshops alone...the scope of this movement must be extended, generalized, the question raised to a general political level, in other

words the movement broadened into a general uprising with the object of overthrowing the bourgeoisie by the seizure of power by the working class.... This is the only way to salvation; otherwise the disintegration and collapse of the mighty and magnificent movement that has begun is inevitable.[11]

None of this had any effect. The PSI failed to give the mass movement an overall political direction, failed to direct it toward the seizure of power, failed to make technical preparations for an insurrection. Inevitably, the predicted "disintegration and collapse" set in. The outcome was disastrous. The thoroughly frightened but still intact ruling class began to turn to fascism. "Mussolini's movement, weak and negligible before September 1920, grew with extraordinary rapidity in the last three months of the year."[12]

The occupation of the factories had proved that the PSI, although affiliated to the Communist International for a year, was not really a communist party. It was symptomatic that Serrati and the bulk of the other maximalist leaders still refused to expel from the party the open reformist tendency led by Turatti—which included, of course, the leaders of the CGL.

After the debacle of September 1920, both the International and the left in the PSI pushed for a split. It came at the PSI's congress in January 1921 held at Livorno. But unlike the splits in the French Socialist Party and the German USPD the previous year, the PSI left did not succeed in winning a majority away from the centrists. The card vote at Livorno was 14,695 for Turatti's open reformists, 58,785 for the left, and 98,028 for Serrati's center group. The left promptly walked out, to form the Italian Communist Party (PCI).

The relationship of forces would not have been so bad if the PCI had an aggressive but flexible strategy for winning the workers who followed Serrati. But it had no such strategy. The dominant force in the PSI left, now the dominant force in the new Communist Party, were the supporters of Amadeo Bordiga. Imposing as a man of iron principle, Bordiga was also an unbendable ultraleft dogmatist. His faction in the PSI had originally been formed on the basis of abstention from parliamentary elections on principle. He had condemned the Turin factory councils as "economistic." Now he was to be absolutely opposed to any united front approach to the Socialist Party.

It was not until the mid-1920s that the hold of the ultralefts on the PCI was finally broken. By then it was too late. Fascism had triumphed.

Germany: the March Action

"The crux of the matter is that Levi in many respects is right politically. Unfortunately he is guilty of a number of breaches of discipline for which the party expelled him. Thalheimer's and Béla Kun's theses are politically utterly fallacious. Mere phrases and playing at Leftism."

Lenin, Letter to Zinoviev, June 6, 1921

IN ITALY in the second half of 1920, a genuine mass revolutionary movement, a movement which could have led to the overthrow of the Italian bourgeois state, to a soviet Italy, and so to a fundamental shift in the balance of power in Europe in favor of the working class, was destroyed by the spinelessness of a centrist party leadership.

In Germany in March 1921, in the absence of a nationwide mass revolutionary movement, a party leadership tried to force the pace, to substitute the party militants for the mass movement. The result was a severe defeat. Not, indeed, a disaster on the Italian scale, but a serious defeat nonetheless, one that was to have a profound and unfavorable influence on the German workers' movement.

There was a connection between the two events. On the surface, it concerned the leadership of the German Communist Party (KPD). Paul Levi, the outstanding KPD leader, had attended the congress of the PSI at Livorno. After the congress, he had criticized the tactical clumsiness of the International's representatives. These were Kristo Kabakchiev, a Bulgarian whom Trotsky described as "a lifeless doctrinaire," and Mátyás Rákosi, a Hungarian "organization man," an "apparatchnik" without a serious political idea in his head who much later (1944–56) was to become the Stalinist boss of Hungary.

Levi's criticisms, which may have been, broadly speaking, correct, led Rákosi to demand an endorsement of his actions and a condemnation of Levi from the German party leadership. He gained his point, by 28 votes to 23. Levi, Clara Zetkin, who was the outstanding women's leader of the KPD and previously of the SPD, Ernst Däumig, who had been a prominent leader of the Berlin shop stewards' movement during the war and was now head of the KPD's "military apparatus," and two other members of the right wing of the party leadership resigned in protest. The left gained a majority.

This shift in the political balance in the KPD "general staff" had important consequences. It gave temporary dominance to a group of lefts—Arkady Maslow, Ruth Fischer, August Thalheimer, Paul Frölich, and others—who believed in the "theory of the offensive": the view that "the working class could be moved only when set in motion by a series of offensive acts," as Fischer put it.[13]

Of the March Action Fischer was later to write: "In the months preceding the Kronstadt revolt in March 1921, an action in Germany to divert the Russian workers from their own troubles had been concocted by a caucus of the Russian party centering around Zinoviev and Béla Kun."[14] It is true enough that Zinoviev and Bukharin were toying with the notion that the German workers might be "galvanized" by an "offensive" undertaken by party militants—and that they were guilty of gross irresponsibility in sending Béla Kun to Germany as Comintern representative with undefined powers. Kun, "my dear Béla," as Lenin said of him, "who also belongs to a poetically gifted nation and considers himself obliged to be constantly more left than left,"[15] was an ardent advocate of the "offensive at all costs." Another Comintern representative, Guralsky (who also went by the name of Kleine), who was reputed to be close to Zinoviev, took the same line. The KPD leadership could reasonably suppose that the Comintern favored the "offensive," although in fact the Comintern executive—which still included Lenin and Trotsky—had taken no such decision. Nevertheless, all the members of the executive bear some responsibility for the actions taken by the KPD leadership, whether responsibility by commission (Zinoviev and Bukharin) or by omission.

But that is only one side of the matter: Kun's adventuristic tendencies met a ready response from the new German leadership. Even the sober Heinrich Brandler was persuaded by Kun. The fact is that among the members of the USPD who had been won to the Communist International after the congress of Halle, there was a strong sentiment for immediate revolutionary action. The lefts, around Maslow and Fischer, gave expression to this impatience, developed a theoretical justification for it, and used it to overthrow their factional opponents in the leadership. These opponents, the group around Levi, were already attempting to direct the party along the lines on which Lenin and Trotsky were to direct the whole International after the Third World Congress. But Levi lacked the authority, the patience, and the tactical skill for this task.

On March 26, 1921, the Social Democratic *Oberpräsident* of Saxony, Otto Hörsing, ordered his police to occupy the Mansfeld copper mines, a communist stronghold, and a number of factories on the pretext that "robbery and looting" were rife. This was almost certainly a calculated provocation. The police and the Social Democratic leaders were well aware that the "offensive" was coming, and Hörsing preferred to deal with it at a time of his own choosing.[16]

The immediate outcome was indeed a rising of sorts, a series of armed clashes between workers and police and soldiers in the Mansfeld region and at the Leuna chemical plants near Halle. Aside from the resources of the KPD's military apparatus, the workers had quantities of arms left over from 1919. For a brief period, Red Guards, led by the anarchist guerrilla Max Hölz, dominated the Mansfeld area. But the action was localized.

This type of situation would have been a difficult one for the most sober party leadership. As in the "July Days" in Petrograd in 1917, the workers in one center were moving to armed insurrection while the mass of the working class was far from any such thought. The problem was to check the most advanced sections, to organize a retreat while minimizing losses—an extremely hard and tricky operation.

The left leaders of the KPD, intoxicated with romantic notions, pursued the opposite course. They called for a general strike and armed actions against the state. The party's military units were ordered to "provoke" the authorities and so "galvanize" the workers. "Several bombs were exploded in Breslau and Halle; several other bombings planned for Berlin did not materialize."[17] When the strike call fell on deaf ears—as, in general, it did—the party militants were ordered to force the workers out.

"The Friedrich-Albert-Hütte in Rheinhausen, owned by Krupp, was the scene of heavy fighting on Thursday," said one party report quoted by Levi, "between communists who occupied the plant and workers who wanted to go to work. Finally, the workers attacked the communists with clubs and forced their way into the plant. Eight men were wounded."[18] There were big clashes in the Hamburg shipyards between social democratic and communist workers. In Berlin, the party attempted to organize the unemployed to seize the plants and keep the workers out! Everywhere, outside a limited area in central Germany where there was real support, a minority of communist-influenced workers acted without, and often against, the mass of the working class.

The inevitable collapse of the adventure was followed by a savage repression. The KPD was outlawed. Membership fell catastrophically to 150,000 or less, and thousands of militants were imprisoned.

Toward the united front

"The most important question before the Communist International today is to win predominating influence over the majority of the working class, and to bring its decisive strata into the struggle. For despite the objectively revolutionary situation...the majority of workers are still not under communist influence."
Resolution of the Third World Congress, 1921

THE COMMUNIST parties originated out of the split in the working-class movement in 1914 and grew in the course of the struggle against the centrist leaders in 1919–20, a struggle that led to further splits. Perhaps inevitably, hostility and contempt for the reformist and centrist leaders tended to spill over into a dangerous lack of regard for the workers who still followed these leaders. The lunacy of the March Action was the danger signal. A sharp turn "to the right" was essential if the International was to avoid increased isolation from the class it was trying to lead.

Trotsky later claimed: "At the Third World Congress, the overwhelming majority called to order those elements in the International whose views involved the danger that the vanguard might, by precipitate action, be shattered against the passivity and immaturity of the working masses, and against the strength of the capitalist state. That was the greatest danger."[19]

In fact, the majority was anything but overwhelming. Certainly the Theses on Tactics are an implicit condemnation of putschism and adventurism as well as of the passive, propagandist variant of ultraleftism. But it was a hard fight to get them adopted.

And on the March Action itself, Lenin's "extreme right flank" had to be content with an equivocal resolution that declared: "The action of last March was forced on the KPD by the government attack on the workers of central Germany.... The KPD committed a number of errors of which the chief one was that it did not clearly understand the defensive nature of the struggle.... The Congress considers the March Action of the KPD as a step forward.... the KPD must in the future better adapt its battle cry to the actual situation...."[20]

This unsatisfactory compromise was, in part, the result of Paul Levi's public attack on the KPD, an attack that led to his expulsion. Levi published a pamphlet, titled *Our Course Against Putschism,* that contained an essentially correct, if exaggerated, criticism of the party leaders written in extremely violent terms ("the greatest Bakunist putsch in history") and which gave the authorities valuable evidence against the party. But the main factor in the compromise was the continuing strength of the lefts. Not until after the congress did the Comintern executive feel strong enough to draw the logical conclusions of the new line and formally spell out its consequences.

In December, the executive declared that it was "of the opinion that the slogan of the Third World Congress of the Communist International, 'To the Masses,' and the interests of the communist movement generally, require the communist parties and the Communist International as a whole *to support the slogan of the united front of the workers* and to take the initiative in this matter."[21] (The emphasis is in the original.)

This, it was made clear, meant a determined attempt to force the leaderships of the reformist and centrist organizations into limited cooperation on concrete issues *by winning their followers for unity in action,* not merely an attempt to draw those followers into action behind the communist parties.

In January 1922, the executive committee of the Comintern called publicly for "the establishment of a united front of all parties supported by the proletariat, regardless of the differences separating them, so long as they are anxious to wage a common fight for the immediate and urgent needs of the proletariat.... No worker, whether communist or social democrat or syndicalist or even a member of the Christian or liberal trade unions, wants his wages further reduced. None wants to work longer hours.... And therefore all must unite in a common front against the employers' offensive."[22]

This was an enormous retreat from the positions of 1919–20. Yet it was essential in the new conditions. The new line itself was fraught with difficulties and dangers, above all the danger of the communist parties losing their revolutionary energy and ability to shift rapidly to the left when the tide turned again, but these dangers were unavoidable.

The united front tactic is more frequently misunderstood than almost any other element of the revolutionary socialist tradition. It is a method *of struggle* for influence and support in a defensive situation and it presupposes the organizational and political independence of the revolutionary organization.

The tactic starts from the assumption that there is a non-revolutionary situation in which only a minority of the working class supports the revolutionaries. This can be altered only on the basis of a rising level of class struggle, involving large numbers of workers, many of whom will support reformist organizations. The united front is a tactic intended to win these workers' support for revolutionary organizations, which it can do under favorable circumstances. It is not a bloc for joint propaganda between revolutionary and reformist organizations but a limited agreement for *action* of some kind.

Trotsky outlined the thinking of the Comintern leadership on the question early in 1922:

> The task of the Communist Party is to lead the proletarian revolution...to achieve it the Communist Party must base itself on the overwhelming majority of the working class.... The party can achieve this only by remaining an absolutely independent

organization with a clear program and strict internal discipline. That is why the party was bound to break ideologically with the reformists and centrists....

After ensuring itself of the complete independence and ideological homogeneity of its ranks, the Communist Party fights for influence over the majority of the working class.... But it is perfectly self-evident that the class life of the proletariat is not suspended during this period preparatory to the revolution. Clashes with the industrialists, with the bourgeoisie, with the state power, on the initiative of one side or the other, run their due course.

In these clashes—insofar as they involve the vital interests of the entire working class, or of its majority, or of this or that section—the working masses sense the need for unity in action, for unity in resisting the onslaught of capitalism or unity in taking the offensive against it. Any party which mechanically counterposes itself to this need of the working class for unity in action will unfailingly be condemned in the minds of the workers.

Consequently the question of the united front is not at all, either in its point of origin or substance, a question of the reciprocal relations between the communist parliamentary fraction and that of the Socialists, or between the Central Committees of the two parties....

The problem of the united front—despite the fact *that a split is inevitable in this epoch between the various political organizations basing themselves on the working class*—grows out of the urgent need to secure for the working class the possibility of a united front in the struggle against capitalism...wherever the Communist Party constitutes a big, organized force, but not the decisive magnitude...it is confronted with the question of the united front in all its acuteness....

Unity of front consequently presupposes our readiness, within certain limits and on specific issues, to correlate in practice our actions with those of the reformist organizations, to the extent that the latter still express today the will of important sections of the embattled proletariat.

But didn't we split with them? Yes, *because we disagree with them on fundamental questions of the working-class movement.*

And yet we seek agreement with them? Yes, in all cases where the masses that follow them are ready to engage in a joint struggle together with the masses that follow us and when they, the reformists, are to a lesser or greater degree compelled to become an instrument of struggle...in many cases and perhaps even in the majority of cases, organizational agreements will be only half-attained or perhaps not at all. But it is necessary that the struggling masses should always be given the opportunity of convincing themselves that the non-achievement of unity in action was not due to our formalistic irreconcilability but to the real lack of will to struggle on the part of the reformists."[23]

There are enormous practical difficulties in applying this approach in any actual appropriate situation. Each such situation is different; each has, inevitably, unique factors. There is no substitute for the "knowledge, experience and…political flair" of which Lenin wrote, in solving complex political problems. The simple reiteration of the formulae will not suffice.

The Comintern parties themselves provided many obstacles right from the start. For the truth was that the Comintern had *not* achieved the "complete independence and ideological homogeneity of its ranks" of which Trotsky wrote. In Italy, the ultraleft around Bordiga resisted the new tactic. In France, it was opposed both by the centrists in the leadership and by the syndicalists, for whom "politics" was essentially separate from militant trade unionism. In Germany, the unrepentant coauthors of the March Action grouped around Ernst Reuter-Friesland, Maslow, and Fischer were a constant thorn in the side of the leadership of Meyer and Thalheimer, who wished to implement the united front tactic and for this were denounced as "soft," "opportunist," and "social democratic."

Nevertheless, the KPD did manage some successes in applying the united front tactic in 1922–23. After the murder of Walther Rathenau, a government minister, by the far right, the KPD demanded that the SPD fight to disarm the paramilitary right and purge the army. It called for the formation of armed workers' groups—the "proletarian hundreds"—which soon involved many noncommunist workers. It set up factory councils to resist the employers' offensive and check spiraling price rises. Constantly the KPD called for joint action against the bosses and the fascist right. By these methods, it not only rebuilt its own forces after the March Action of 1921 but spread its influence far into the organizations of the working class.

For theory and practice, two things stand out concerning the united front tactic. First, a revolutionary minority party cannot *simply* carry out propaganda and agitation from the fringes of the working-class movement—though it *must* do these things too. Second, the united front tactic is concerned with *working-class* struggles, *working-class* organizations (however reactionary), and is *fundamentally* different *in princi-*

ple from "popular fronts" or "broad democratic alliances." These two central points will be reinforced by later experience of the 1930s.

The Fourth World Congress

"The existence of independent communist parties and their complete freedom of action in regard to the bourgeoisie and the counterrevolutionary social democracy is the most significant historical achievement of the proletariat, which communists will in no circumstances whatever renounce. Only communist parties fight for the interests of the proletariat in its entirety. Nor does the united front tactic mean so-called upper level 'electoral alliances' which pursue some parliamentary purpose or other. The united front tactic is the offer of a joint struggle of communists with all workers who belong to other parties or groups, and with all nonparty workers, in the defense of the basic interests of the working class against the bourgeoisie.... The most important thing in the united front tactic is and remains the agitational and organizational rallying of the working masses. Its true realization can only come 'from below,' from the depths of the working masses themselves. Communists, however, must not refuse in certain circumstances to negotiate with the leaders of hostile workers' parties, but the masses must be kept fully and constantly informed of the course of these negotiations. Nor must the communist parties' freedom to agitate be circumscribed in any way during these negotiations with the leaders."

Theses on Tactics, Adopted by the Fourth World Congress of the Communist International, December 1922

THE FOURTH World Congress, held in November–December 1922, was the last Comintern Congress that Lenin attended (and he was already too sick to participate save for one speech). It was also the last congress that the subsequent Trotskyist tradition accepted as a genuinely revolutionary communist congress.

What had been achieved since the first congress? Capitalism had weathered the storms of 1919–20, with the indispensable aid of the social democrats and centrists. Nevertheless, substantial revolutionary workers' parties now existed in a number of important European countries. The parties, typically, led only minorities in the working class, as was natural during the ebb tide, but they were big enough in many cases to be a serious factor. Hence the relevance of the united front tactic. The potential for seizing the opportunities that future revolutionary situations would open up was incomparably greater than in 1919. The 343 voting delegates at the congress from fifty-eight countries represented the most powerful revolutionary workers' movement there had ever been.

Naturally, like every living mass movement, it had plenty of defects and deformations. It suffered from internal conflicts that reflected, in the last resort, the pressure of alien and hostile social forces. It suffered too from the internal conflicts derived from immaturity, from the lack of stable, authoritative national revolutionary leaderships, evolved and tested in action and enjoying the confidence of the mass of the members and of at least some workers beyond the membership. The overwhelming authority of the international leadership, of Lenin, Trotsky, Zinoviev, and indeed of all the Russians, overshadowed everyone else.

This authority was not yet based on manipulation, bureaucratic maneuvers, or even the voting strength of the Russian Communist Party. It was based on the obvious fact that not only had the Russians "made their revolution" but that they had been correct—and had eventually been seen to be correct in the eyes of most responsible militants—in the disputes inside the Comintern since 1919. Correct against the ultralefts, whose victory would have reduced the movement to a sect. Correct against the centrists, whose victory would have dragged it back into a left social democratic swamp. Without the prestige of the Russian Revolution, and therefore of Lenin and his associates, the Comintern could not have become a mass organization, if indeed it could have existed at all in any serious sense.

But this situation contained the seeds of a very obvious danger. It was one thing to "go to school" under the Russians but quite another to come to rely on the teachers to solve the complex problems facing the German, Polish, British, U.S., or whatever parties. The teaching that the Russians could give from their own revolutionary experience was the best available in the early years. But an important objective of any real education is to emancipate the pupil from excessive dependence on the teacher. Lenin recognized the danger. The only speech he was able to make at the fourth congress contains this passage:

> At the third congress, we adopted a resolution on the organizational structure of the Communist Parties and on the methods and content of their activities. The resolution is an excellent one, but it is almost entirely Russian, that is to say, because it is too Russian. Not because it is written in Russian—it has been excellently translated into all languages—but no foreigner can read it. I have read it again before saying this.
>
> In the first place, it is too long, containing fifty or more points. Foreigners are not usually able to read such things. Secondly, even if they read it, they will not understand it because it is too Russian. Not because it is written in Russian—it has been excellently translated into all languages—but because it is thoroughly imbued with the Russian spirit. And thirdly, if by way of exception some foreigner does understand it, he cannot carry it out. This is its third defect. I have the impression that we made a big mistake with this resolution, namely, that we blocked our own road to further successes.... All that we said in the resolution has remained a dead letter. If we do not realize this, we shall be unable to move ahead.[24]

In retrospect, it is clear that the problem lay much deeper than this, much deeper than Lenin himself realized. The more the influence of the Russians was reinforced, the greater became the dependence of the international movement on the outcome of the postrevolutionary struggle for power in a backward and isolated country in which the working class itself was disintegrating.

Yet the leadership of the Russian Communist Party was still incomparably superior in 1922 to the leaderships of the European parties. It further reinforced its authority in the 1922–23 struggles against the leaders of the French and Norwegian parties.

Herein lies the tragedy of the subsequent development of the Comintern. The complex process of uneven and combined development of both capitalism and of the workers' movements had not only falsified the assumption made by Marx and Engels that the workers' revolution would occur first in what were, in their day, the most economically and politically developed countries—Britain, France, and Germany—it had also led to Russian dominance of the revolutionary movement at the very moment when workers' power was dying of atrophy in Russia itself.

For already in 1921, speaking in support of the New Economic Policy (NEP), Lenin had argued that "owing to the war and to the desperate poverty and ruin [the proletariat] has been declassed, i.e., dislodged from its class groove, and has ceased to exist as a proletariat.... Since large-scale capitalist industry has been destroyed, since the factories are at a standstill, the proletariat has disappeared. It has sometimes figured in the statistics, but it has not held together economically."[25]

The Moscow in which the delegates gathered was already ruled by a bureaucracy, still controlled at the top by a thin layer of revolutionaries, but essentially a substitute for workers' power.

The fourth congress took various decisions extending and developing the united front tactic. It adopted "the slogan of a workers' government (or a workers' and peasants' government)" to be "used practically everywhere as a general propaganda slogan,"[26] which meant that "Communists are prepared to act together with those workers who have not yet recognized the necessity of the proletarian dictatorship, social democrats, members of Christian parties, nonparty syndicalists, etc. They are thus ready, in certain circumstances and with certain guarantees, to support a workers' government that is not communist."[27]

There was already an important precedent for this. Before the congress of Halle and in the immediate aftermath of the Kapp Putsch in 1920, Karl Legien, the extreme right-wing leader of the ADGB—the German trade union federation—had proposed an alliance of the SPD, the USPD, and the unions to fight for a "workers' government" to "republicanize" the German state machine by purging right-wing officers in the army and the civil service, and to carry out limited social reforms, including a land reform to break the power of the Prussian Junkers—the landowning aristocracy—and nationalization of the mines.

The KPD, then still only fifty thousand to sixty thousand strong, was drawn into the negotiations. Legien wanted them involved because of their influence on the insurgent workers of Saxony and the Ruhr who were effectively in power in a number of places. The proposal put to the KPD was that they should give "critical support" to such a government, while preserving their freedom of action in other respects. "Critical support" involved rejection of any immediate armed struggle against the Weimar Republic and against the proposed "workers' government."

Paul Levi, then the dominant leader of the KPD, and his representatives in the negotiations, Jakob Walcher and Wilhelm Pieck, were in favor of such an agreement. The party as a whole regarded it as little less than treason.

Who was right? Unquestionably, the agreement should have been seized with both hands. The SPD leaders had been badly shaken by the Kapp Putsch, which was the result of their support for the creation of the Reichswehr (the new professional German Army). They were losing ground fast to the left (mainly to the USPD). At the same time, the mass of the twelve million and more workers who had actively resisted and defeated the putsch had done so in defense of the Weimar Republic. The argument that that republic, under new leadership, might really crush the far right and solve at least some of the problems of working people needed to be tested in practice—not to convince the communist militants of course, but to convince the mass of the working class. For naturally, an SPD-USPD government would have failed to live up to the prospectus. So much the better for the KPD. For, it must be stressed, there was never any question of KPD participation in the "workers' government."

In the event, the whole scheme came to nothing and the congress of Halle, which resulted in the splitting of the USPD and a mass influx of members into the KPD, transformed the situation for the party. Nevertheless, Levi and his associates were right. The KPD was a small minority before the Halle congress and still a minority, though now a large one, after it. Armed struggle would therefore have been adventurism. The KPD had first to win the decisive sections of the working class—and critical support of a "workers' government" in the sense indicated, could have greatly facilitated this process.

The negotiations with Legien preceded by a year the adoption of the slogan "To the Masses" and the united front tactic by the Third World Congress. At the fourth congress, the matter was taken much further. It is useful to consider the congress resolution in some detail. After the statement about the use of the idea of a "workers' government" "as a general propaganda slogan," it continues:

> But as a topical political slogan, it is of the greatest importance in those countries where bourgeois society is particularly unstable, where the relation of forces between the workers' parties and the bourgeoisie is such that the decision of the question, who shall form the government, becomes one of immediate practical necessity. In these countries, the slogan of a workers' government follows inevitably from the entire united front tactic.
>
> The parties of the Second International are trying to "save" the situation by advocating and forming a coalition government of bourgeois and social democratic parties.... To this open or concealed bourgeois–social democratic coalition, the communists oppose the united front of all workers and a coalition of all workers' parties in the economic and the political field for the fight against the bourgeois power and its eventual overthrow. In the united struggle of all workers against the bourgeoisie, the entire state apparatus must be taken over by the workers' government, and thus the working class's position of power strengthened.
>
> The overriding tasks of the workers' government must be to arm the workers, to disarm bourgeois and counterrevolutionary organizations, to introduce workers' control of production, to transfer the main burden of taxation to the rich, and to break the resistance of the counterrevolutionary bourgeoisie. Such a workers' government is only possible if it is born out of the struggle of the masses, is supported by workers' bodies which are capable of fighting, bodies created by the most oppressed sections of the working masses.[28]

The purpose of the slogan of the "workers' government" was "concentrating the proletariat and unleashing revolutionary struggles."[29] In a situation such as that immediately following the Kapp Putsch, it might well contribute to such an outcome, always provided that it was a matter of critical support for a workers' government by an independent communist party. However, the resolution went much further.

It envisaged communist party participation "in certain circumstances" in a "workers' government." True, such participation was hedged around with various qualifications, but the thing is clearly wrong in principle. Indeed, some of the qualifications make it worse: "Only if there are guarantees that the workers' government will really struggle against the bourgeoisie in the sense mentioned"—if social democrats and centrists could do that ("arm the workers...break the resistance of the counterrevolutionary bourgeoisie"), they would cease to be reformists. Moreover, notwithstanding the talk of "the struggle of the masses," the slogan of the workers' government inevitably shifted the emphasis to the question of parliamentary majorities—and was so interpreted in Germany in 1923.

In 1921, the opposition to the united front tactic had come mainly from the ultraleft. In 1922–23, it came mainly from the right, from the centrist and left reformist tendencies that still had a sizeable foothold in a number of communist parties. It came too, in deeds rather than words, from what can best be described as "neo-Kautskian" tendencies—tendencies derived from pre-1914 Kautskianism, which meant abstract revolutionism, the belief that socialism would result from "inevitable" historical tendencies and a passive approach to the class struggle.

In France, the centrist group led by Frossard seized on opposition to the tactic of the united front as a means of rallying opposition to "Moscow" and for "autonomy." In reality, their opposition was to the building of a revolutionary party in their own country. They opposed an active, aggressive attempt to involve the rank and file of the Socialist Party in action precisely because they were moving ever closer to the Socialist Party leaders.

As Trotsky shrewdly noted:

> On the question of the united front we see the very same passive and irresolute tendency, but this time marked by verbal irreconcilability. At the very first glance, one is hit between the eyes by the following paradox: the rightist party elements with their centrist and pacifist tendencies, who overtly or covertly support *Journal du Peuple,* come simultaneously to the forefront as the most irreconcilable opponents of the united front, covering themselves with the banner of revolutionary intransigence. In contrast, those elements who have right up to the Tours Convention held in the most difficult hours the position of the Third International are today in favor of the united front. As a matter of fact, the mask of pseudo-revolutionary intransigence is now being assumed by the partisans of the dilatory and passive tactic.[30]

The Frossard faction won a majority at the party congress held in October 1922, although a narrow one. The representatives of the Comintern executive committee at the congress, Humbert Droz and Dmitry Manuilsky, argued for parity on the leading bodies between left and right. When this was rejected, they acted in the spirit of the view held by the majority of the Comintern executive of the time and summarized in Zinoviev's slogan "peace is better"—in other words, avoid new splits at almost any cost—and bent all their efforts to force the left to submit.

"The Left received orders from Manuilsky to bow to the decision.... But the orders showed a misunderstanding of the temper of the Right. Frossard meant to exploit...[his victory] to the full. All posts in the party were filled by nominees of the Right."[31]

Frossard and his associates used this success to prepare to split the party and lead it back to unity with the reformist minority. In the event Frossard precipitated the split in January 1923. Though he took with him "most of the 'politicians,' journalists, municipal councilors and the like,"[32] the bulk of the working-class membership remained loyal and the communist party gained in membership after the split. Frossard subsequently became general secretary of the (reformist) SFIO.

In Norway, the outcome was less favorable. The centrist leaders Martin Tranmael and Trygre Lie (subsequently first secretary-general of the "United Nations Organization") had been preparing a break since the summer of 1920 but had skillfully delayed it, even though this required that the DNA accept the Comintern's twenty-one conditions (in words) until the revolutionary tide was clearly ebbing away.

Tranmael and Lie forced a split by 169 votes to 110 at the 1923 congress, ostensibly on the familiar issue of "autonomy," and took the majority of the membership. But the DNA still faced, until the late 1920s, a substantial communist party. The DNA got 18 percent of the vote and twenty-four deputies elected in the 1924 election, while the Norwegian Communist Party got 6 percent and six deputies.[33] More important, the Communist Party took a good part of the organized working-class base. But unlike the French Communist Party, the Norwegian party was a minority from its inception, even among organized workers. Tranmael and the DNA held the majority of organized workers on a centrist basis, talking left but moving rightwards. They did not join the reconstituted reformist International and continued to "talk left" until the moment came for them to form His Norwegian Majesty's government in 1936.

International maneuvers

"The representatives of the Second and Two-and-a-Half Internationals need a united front, for they hope to weaken us by inducing us to make exorbitant concessions; they hope to penetrate into our communist premises without any payment; they hope to utilize united front tactics for the purpose of convincing the workers that reformist tactics are correct and that revolutionary tactics are wrong. We need a united front because we hope to convince the workers of the opposite."

Lenin, We Have Paid Too Much, April 1922

AT BERNE, in February 1919, the congress intended to constitute the Second International assembled, shorn of many of its former affiliates—the Belgians refused to attend because they would not sit with Germans, the Italians and Swiss would not sit with the anti-Zimmerwald parties, the Bolsheviks were violently hostile, and so on.

Some of the centrists, notably the USPD, did attend, but essentially this was a congress of the right-wing rump of the old International. It was paralyzed by the "war-guilt" issue; the attempt of the French right wing to fasten exclusive responsibility for the war on the Central Powers—and so to condemn only German and Austrian social democrats for supporting the war—along the lines of the infamous "war-guilt" clause of the Versailles Treaty. The congress was reduced to setting up an action committee "to reestablish the International in the shortest possible time,"[34] in other words to reunite the right, which was riven by national differences, against the revolutionaries.

By the time this body was able to convene another congress, at Lucerne in August 1919, the Communist International had been founded and the revolutionary tide was flowing strongly in Europe. Eighteen parties were present (there had been twenty-three at Berne) and there was a big apparent shift to the left. No more was heard of German "war guilt." Indeed, the whole Versailles Treaty was condemned outright, as was allied military intervention against the Russian and Hungarian revolutions.

But these verbal concessions to the left failed to keep the centrists in the right-wing fold. Under growing pressure from their radicalized memberships, the French (now under centrist leadership), Austrian, U.S., Norwegian, and Spanish parties, as well as the USPD, all broke from the reconstituted Second International before its Geneva congress in July 1920. A new centrist international, the "Two-and-a-Half International" or Vienna Union, came into being—formally constituted in February 1921. Its core was the Austrian social democratic party, the leaders of which had avoided any sizeable split to the left by covering their support for the re-creation of the bourgeois state in Austria (in the form of a bourgeois democratic republic) by revolutionary rhetoric.

Essentially the Two-and-a-Half International was an attempt to repeat this maneuver on a European scale, to prevent further gains for the Communist International and to pull back as many as possible of those who had gone over to it in 1920. The Vienna Union's watchword was "unity." The post-Halle USPD, the post-Tours SFIO, the British ILP, and the Russian Mensheviks all took part. Altogether it was claimed that twenty parties in thirteen countries adhered to the Vienna Union.

In January 1922, the Bureau of the Two-and-a-Half International issued a call for a "general international conference of the class-conscious world proletariat."[35] The executive committee of the Comintern at once agreed to participate. The executive of the revived Second International raised a series of difficulties, which were intended to torpedo the conference, but, in the event, it was compelled to attend by fear of further losses to the left.

The conference eventually assembled in the Reichstag building in Berlin (by courtesy of the SPD) in April 1922. Clara Zetkin, for the Comintern, rejected any idea of "organic unity," of a single International, as proposed by the "two-and-a-halfers," but put forward the theme of "a common defense against the attacks of world capitalism."[36]

Naturally, the delegates of the Second International—prominent among whom was James Ramsay MacDonald, future Labor and then Tory prime minister of Britain—were not

interested in that. They insisted on debating the issue of Cau-
casian Georgia, where a Menshevik government originally established under British military protection had just been
overthrown by the Red Army, the issue of the trial of counter-
revolutionaries in Russia, and so on.

Concessions by the Comintern delegation, which Lenin
later denounced as impermissible, prevented the immediate
breakup of the conference but the "two-and-a-halfers" soon
came to an understanding with the right. Together they con-
vened another conference that excluded the communists, at
which they fused their forces to form a Labor and Socialist International in May 1923. This body maintained a paper existence until 1939 when it collapsed ignominiously with the
outbreak of the Second World War.

There were also the two trade union Internationals. The International Federation of Trade Unions (IFTU) had been set up
in 1913, largely as a gesture of independence from party control, by the very right-wing leadership of the German trade
union federation (ADGB). It collapsed the next year when each
of its two biggest constituents (the British TUC and the German
ADGB) backed its "own" government on the outbreak of war.

The IFTU was reestablished at a congress at Amsterdam in
July 1919. It was a stronghold of the right, the European right-
wingers being reinforced by the strongly antisocialist American
Federation of Labor. The founding congress claimed to represent nearly eighteen million trade unionists: "This so-called
Trade Union International does, unfortunately, represent something," said Zinoviev in 1920, "in fact it is the bulwark of the
international bourgeoisie."[37]

The Red International of Labor Unions (known as the
Profintern) was intended partly as a counterweight to the
IFTU, partly as a means of drawing the syndicalist union federations of France (CGT) and Spain (CNT) and smaller groups
elsewhere into a closer relationship with the Comintern.

The tenth of the twenty-one conditions that were required
of every party affiliating to the Comintern had stipulated "an
unyielding struggle against the Amsterdam 'International' of
yellow trade unions." Each party "must conduct the most vigorous propaganda among trade unionists for the necessity of a
break with the yellow Amsterdam International. It must do all

it can to support the international association of red trade unions, adhering to the Communist International, which is being formed."[38]

It was not until July 1921 that the Red International of Labor Unions was able to hold its founding congress: the Italian, Bulgarian, and Norwegian union federations attended, together with the Russians and a number of smaller organizations. It was claimed that the 380 delegates from forty-one countries represented "seventeen million out of a total of forty million trade unionists all over the world,"[39] an extremely dubious claim. But by this time, with the ebbing of the revolutionary tide, the united front tactic was coming to the fore and it is questionable whether the formation of the Red International was a useful operation in the circumstances.

Three years later, Zinoviev admitted: "Profintern was founded at a moment when it seemed that we should break through the enemy front in a frontal attack and quickly conquer the trade unions.... It was a moment when we thought we should quite quickly win the majority of the workers."[40]

Factually, this is inaccurate. It expresses the perspective of 1920, not that of the summer of 1921, but it very obviously represented the thinking behind the original decision to attempt to confront and defeat the IFTU on its own ground.

In the end, although the Italian union federation was shortly to be smashed by the fascists and the Norwegians were soon to secede, some more flesh was put on the Profintern skeleton by the splits in the French and Czechoslovak trade union movements.

The CGT, the only significant French union organization, had adopted a revolutionary syndicalist position in 1906 (embodied in the *Carte d'Amiens*). The war proved that hostility to socialist parties rightly suspected of reformism—which was the essence of the syndicalist position—in no way guaranteed that the syndicalists would remain independent from the capitalist state. The CGT itself rapidly developed pro-war reformist and antiwar revolutionary trends together with a temporarily majority "center" tendency that was pro-Zimmerwald but anti-Bolshevik.

The right wing, seeing that the combined forces of left and center were gaining a substantial majority, split the CGT after its Lille congress (July 1921) and stole the name and most of the full-time apparatus, thus forcing the left to set up the CGTU in June 1922. At that time, the CGTU commanded the support of the majority of organized workers in France and its affiliation to the Red International was a serious blow to the IFTU. It also modified the Red International itself. The syndicalist majority wing of the CGTU leadership insisted, successfully, on the removal of Comintern nominees from the Red International executive.

The next year, the Czech chauvinist right-wing bosses of the Czechoslovak union federation expelled unions that organized the majority of trade unionists in Czechoslovakia. The expelled left established the Multinational Trade Union Center—multinational referring to the German, Slovak, Ruthenian, Hungarian, and Polish minorities that, together, constituted a majority of the population of the state of Czechoslovakia that had been created by the Treaty of Versailles at the end of the First World War. The Multinational Trade Union Center now affiliated to the Red International.

The Spanish CNT, however, eventually rejected both Amsterdam and Moscow. Its anarcho-syndicalist wing won a decisive victory at a congress in Saragossa in June 1922, which voted to adhere to a syndicalist international, the AIT, of which the CNT remained the only significant affiliate.

The Red International had, from the beginning, fought against the ultraleft notion that individuals or groups of communist sympathizers should secede from IFTU unions. Its first congress resolved: "This tactic of the withdrawal of revolutionary elements from the unions...plays into the hands of the counterrevolutionary trade union bureaucracy and therefore should be sharply and categorically rejected."[41]

A little later, it was decided that individual unions in federations affiliated to the Amsterdam IFTU should not be encouraged to secede. Nevertheless, the very existence of the Red International made more difficult the necessary task of fighting for trade union unity, even though this was the official platform of the Red International. The fight for the slogan of trade union unity—"in those countries where two parallel trade union centers are in existence (Spain, France, Czechoslovakia, etc.), communists must begin a systematic struggle for re-union of these parallel organizations"[42]—was hardly helped by the existence of an international parallel center, which inevitably developed its own self-justifying inertia and apparatus.

The Fourth World Congress of the Comintern repeated the call for unity—which "makes it the duty of every communist party to do everything in its power to prevent the splitting of the trade unions, to restore the unity of the trade union movement where it has been destroyed"[43]—and also took up the question of "autonomy," the syndicalist watchword.

Bourgeois influence on the proletariat is expressed in the theory of neutrality: the trade unions are to stick to purely craft, narrowly economic aims, and not general class aims.... The bourgeoisie always tend to separate politics from economics for they realize very well that if they manage to confine the working class within the frame of craft interests, their rule is not seriously endangered. The same frontier between economics and politics is drawn by the anarchist elements in the trade union movement in order to divert the workers' movement from the political path on the pretext that all politics are directed against the workers. This theory, in essence purely bourgeois, is presented to the workers as the theory of trade union autonomy, which is then interpreted as hostility of the trade unions to the communist parties and as a declaration of war on the communist workers' movement, still on the notorious pretext of independence and autonomy.[44]

This was a shrewd diagnosis. Events soon proved decisively that syndicalist union bureaucrats, notably those of the French CGT and the Spanish CNT, were every bit as hostile to initiatives from below and the communist influence as their social-democratic counterparts. Autonomism, which had a revolutionary (or more commonly pseudo-revolutionary) content before 1914, became reactionary after the best syndicalist militants went over to the Comintern and the remaining syndicalist leaders came to see it as their most dangerous opponent.

FOUR

1923: THE CRUCIAL YEAR

"Of course, the weaknesses of the communist parties and of their leadership did not fall from the sky, but are rather a product of the entire past of Europe. But the communist parties could develop at a swift pace in the present existing maturity of the objectively revolutionary contradictions provided, of course, there was a correct leadership on the part of the Comintern, speeding up this process of development instead of retarding it."

Trotsky, *Strategy and Tactics in the Imperialist Epoch*

IN 1923, the interlinked fates of the revolutionary regime in Russia and of the Communist International stood poised on a knife-edge. In Russia (the USSR from the turn of the year), the increasingly bureaucratic regime drifted. It was, as the historian E. H. Carr noted, "a sort of intermediate period—a truce or interregnum in party and Soviet affairs—when controversial decisions were, so far as possible, avoided or held in suspense."[1]

The bureaucracy had not yet crystallized into a self-conscious layer. No one yet ventured to speak of "socialism in one country"; but, as Lenin had said the previous year,

> The state is in our hands; but has it operated the New Economic Policy in the way we wanted in this past year? No. But we refuse to admit that it did not operate in the way we wanted. How did it operate? The machine refused to obey the hand that guided it. It was like a car that was not going in the direction the driver desired, but in the direction someone else desired; as if it were being driven by some mysterious, lawless hand, God knows whose, perhaps of a profiteer, or of a private capitalist, or both. Be that as it may, the car is not going

quite in the direction the man at the wheel imagines, and often it goes in an altogether different direction.[2]

The "mysterious, lawless hand" was the product of the immensely powerful social forces generated in Russia by industrial decline, desperately low productivity of labor, cultural backwardness, and general scarcity. Because these social forces—the forces of reaction, of the Russian "Thermidor"— had not yet found an effective political expression, the outcome was far from decided in 1923. The rulers acted "consciously indeed, yet with a sort of false consciousness," as Marx had once written of earlier historical actors. None of them fully understood what was happening.

The term "Thermidor" was familiar to the majority of the Comintern leadership. They had, of course, studied the great French Revolution of 1789–94, the classic bourgeois revolution. On July 27, 1794, which was the ninth Thermidor according to the French revolutionary calendar, the Jacobin dictatorship was overthrown and replaced by a rightward-moving government that took the title of the Directory in the following year. This led eventually to a *social* reaction and to the dictatorship of Napoleon Bonaparte.

"Thermidor" was a much-used term in the controversies of the 1920s in Russia. Was this what was happening in Russia? If so, what was its class basis? These questions were still open in 1923. But the *threat* of a Thermidor was apparent, and leftist trends in the Russian and German communist parties were already speculating about it. So what *was* happening in the leaderships of the Comintern and the Russian Communist Party?

Lenin was no longer "the man at the wheel." His health had given way in December 1921, and recovery was never more than partial. In May 1922, he suffered a paralyzing stroke that temporarily deprived him of speech. Two further strokes followed in December that year. A fourth, in March 1923, ended his political life, though he did not die physically until January 1924. Consequently, he was entirely without influence on the direction of the Comintern in 1923, a fact of considerable importance, since no one else had his combination of immense authority and profound grasp of the dynamics of revolution.

The regeneration of the Russian Revolution—after the destruction of Russia's industrial base in the years of war, civil war, famine, and foreign intervention that had decimated the working class—was now desperately needed. This regeneration now depended more than ever on events outside Russia; above all, on events in Germany. It depended therefore on the maturity and political ability of the leaderships of the European communist parties, especially of the KPD, and on the ability of the Comintern center to aid and guide them.

At the Comintern's Fourth World Congress, the machinery of the center was considerably elaborated. Provision was made for meetings once every four months of an "enlarged executive" with representatives from all the communist parties, supplementing the twenty-five members of the Comintern executive committee. A presidium was set up on the pattern of the Russian Politburo, plus an organization bureau, an agit-prop department, a statistical department, and others. None of this improved the *political* effectiveness of the Comintern executive.

The decisive role continued to be played by three Russian party members: Zinoviev, Bukharin, and Radek. It was not a combination whose record should have inspired confidence: Zinoviev and Bukharin had countenanced the lunacy of the March Action in Germany, while Zinoviev had also opposed the October insurrection in Russia in 1917. Radek was clever but, as Lenin said, "boneless."

True, this combination had been in office in the Comintern since 1919—but with a difference. "Under Lenin," Trotsky wrote some years later, "the *immediate* leadership of the affairs of the International was entrusted to Zinoviev, Radek, and Bukharin. In the solution of all questions of any great substance, Lenin and the author of these lines took part. Needless to say, in all fundamental questions of the International, the key was in the hands of Lenin."[3] Now Lenin was wholly incapacitated, and Trotsky, as events were to show, was unable to exert the same influence that he had previously, with Lenin's support.

Nevertheless, the outcome of the events of 1923 cannot simply be attributed to the actions of the Comintern center. This was far from all-powerful. The political weaknesses of the leaderships of the Bulgarian and German communist parties were still more important. It was the combination of weakness in the field and at the headquarters that proved fatal.

The lack of a politically trained cadre, schooled by experience, in the non-Russian parties, was the decisive weakness. It could not be rectified in short order then. Today we can, with the wisdom of hindsight, develop such a cadre—if we can learn the lessons.

Defeat in Bulgaria

"The armed struggle between the followers of the fallen government and those of the new government is not yet at an end. The Communist Party, and the hundreds of thousands of workers and peasants united beneath its flag, are not taking part in this struggle.... It is a struggle for power between the bourgeoisies of the city and of the village, that is, between two wings of the capitalist class."

Statement of the Central Committee of the Bulgarian
Communist Party, June 11, 1923 (emphasis added)

ON JUNE 9, 1923 the Bulgarian army and police, encouraged by the leaders of right-wing political parties and supported by the armed units of the Macedonian nationalist organization, the IMRO, launched a coup d'état against the Peasant Union Party government of Alexander Stambulisky. In the fighting that followed, the Bulgarian Communist Party not only proclaimed its neutrality in what it called "a struggle between two wings of the capitalist class" but repudiated and disciplined the communists of Plevna district who had spontaneously joined the resistance to the coup.

It was a repetition, but worse, of the initial reaction of the leaders of the KPD to the Kapp Putsch in Germany. Worse because it was not reversed under pressure from the ranks; worse because the Bulgarian party, unlike the KPD, was not an infant but had existed since 1903.

Tsankov, the leader of the coup, helped by this passivity, succeeded in crushing the resistance of Stambulisky's Peasant Union. He established a military regime, decorated with representatives of the bourgeois parties, and, it should be noted, the Bulgarian social democrats.

The leaders of the Bulgarian Communist Party were not opportunists and they were not cowards. They had resolutely opposed the imperialist world war, withstanding persecution and imprisonment. Nor were they, in the everyday sense, incompetents. They had built a mass movement and marginalized the social democrats.

Some idea of the balance of forces is given by the results of the local elections of January 1923, which were, by Balkan standards, free elections. "The Peasant Union secured 437,000 votes or rather less than half the total poll; next came the Bulgarian Communist Party with 230,000; the bourgeois parties taken together could muster only 220,000, and the 'broad' (or right-wing) socialists no more than 40,000."[4] In the general election that followed in April, and which the opposition parties denounced as marked by intimidation and manipulation, the Communist Party was still credited with 210,000 votes to the Peasant Union's 500,000. The Communist Party had 39,000 members, a sizeable number in a country of fewer than five million people, and controlled most of the admittedly weak trade unions.

Why then did the Communist Party fail to act in the crisis of June 1923? In January, the party had endorsed the call for a workers' and peasants' government—about four-fifths of the population were peasants—but had declared: "The workers' and peasants' government cannot today in Bulgaria be realized through a coalition of the Communist Party with the Peasant Union or through a peasant government resulting from such a coalition."[5]

This was certainly correct. Insofar as the elastic slogan calling for a workers' and peasants' government could be given a revolutionary content, this could only be through the splitting of a peasant party in the course of a revolution—as had happened in Russia at the end of 1917, when the Bolsheviks had formed a coalition soviet government with the left wing of the peasant Socialist Revolutionary Party.

The leader of the Bulgarian Communist Party, Kabakchiev, was entirely correct in describing the Peasant Union as dominated by rich peasants (kulaks) and the rural bourgeoisie. He had rightly declared: "The workers' and peasants' government can be created only through the revolutionary struggle of the masses, that is, through the independent struggle of the urban proletariat and of the small and landless peasants."[6] But this impeccably orthodox analysis had no relevance at all to the question of the Tsankov coup.

In August 1917, the Bolsheviks in Russia had thrown all their forces into the fight against General Kornilov when he attempted a coup against the Kerensky government. At the time, that same government was persecuting the Bolsheviks, had driven Lenin into exile, and thrown Trotsky into prison. It was itself half in league with Kornilov. But all this had not prevented the Bolsheviks from grasping the main fact: that a victory for Kornilov would be a massive defeat for the working class and for the prospects of revolution.

The Bolsheviks, however, did not give *political* support to Kerensky. As Lenin put it:

> We shall fight, we are fighting against Kornilov *just as Kerensky's troops do,* but we do not support Kerensky. *On the contrary,* we expose his weakness.... *At the moment,* we must campaign not so much directly against Kerensky, as *indirectly* against him, namely, by demanding a more and more active, truly revolutionary, war against Kornilov. The development of this war alone can lead *us* to power.[7]

This did indeed happen in Russia. Whether the same result could have been obtained in Bulgaria remained untested. The Bulgarian Communist Party *abstained* in the struggle, a policy guaranteed to lead to disaster. Its leaders had failed to learn from the experience of the Bolsheviks against Kornilov, or from the Kapp Putsch in Germany. They were so concerned to maintain their political independence from Stambulisky that they fell into passivity and ignored the main danger—Tsankov. Not for nothing had Trotsky called Kabakchiev a "lifeless doctrinaire." Failure to evaluate the realities of a new situation was at the root of the Bulgarian disaster.

The Comintern executive, meeting from June 12 onward, took a correct position. The Bulgarian party, said Zinoviev, "must ally themselves with the peasantry and even with the hated Stambulisky in order to organize a common struggle against the Whites."[8] Yet even at this thirteenth hour, the Bulgarian communists stuck to their line with a tenacity that would have been admirable in a better cause.

The Bulgarian Communist Party Council issued this statement early in July:

The council of the party completely approves of the attitude adopted by the party central committee to the events of June 9...which...was the only possible one under the circumstances. The party council is of the opinion that the differences of opinion with respect to the tactics of the party on the occasion of the coup d'état between the Comintern executive...and the Communist Party of Bulgaria are to be attributed to the inadequate information of the Comintern executive on the events of June 9.... With respect to the appeal made by the Comintern executive to the working masses, in which these are summoned to join forces with the leaders of the Peasant Union, the party council is of the opinion that...it would be an error for the Communist Party to restore to the agrarian leaders, who have betrayed the interests of the rural working people, their lost influence.[9]

Of course, life itself, not to mention the pressure of the Comintern, soon made this position untenable. The Tsankov government, once having disposed of Peasant Union resistance, turned the full weight of repression against the Communist Party.

After sharp internal conflict, the party leadership shifted toward a united front approach in August 1923, correctly but far too late. Unfortunately, it did not stop at that. Having missed the tide in June, it now, with the workers and peasants disorganized and in retreat, prepared its own March Action. It planned an armed rising, originally for October, then for September 22.

It was a disaster. Tsankov, getting wind of the plan, struck first with mass arrests. Scattered risings broke out between the 19th and the 28th but they were smashed within days. There had been no serious political preparations and the situation was highly unfavorable. The rising was pure adventurism. It was followed by a White terror vastly worse than anything that had gone before.

The September disaster in Bulgaria, unlike that in June, was not homegrown. The Zinoviev-Bukharin leadership of the Comintern presidium had urged it. Although the Comintern's public manifesto in June had spoken only in general terms— "The putschists are now *the* enemy, and must be defeated. Unite for the fight against the White revolt"—Zinoviev's envoy Kolarov had brought much more specific directives in August that led to the attempted rising.

And after the event, the critics of the attempted rising were removed from the Bulgarian leadership—and later mostly expelled—whereas Kolarov and Dimitrov, the advocates of un-questioning obedience, were installed as the Moscow-approved leadership in exile.

The German October

"In the latter part of the last year, we witnessed in Germany a classic demonstration of how it is possible to miss a perfectly exceptional revolutionary situation of world-historic importance."

Trotsky, *Lessons of October*, 1924

AT ITS Jena congress in August 1921, the KPD had endorsed the tactic of the united front, against the opposition of its left wing, and had adopted a program of partial demands. Quick results could hardly be expected in this immediate aftermath of the March Action, but in the following summer a considerable success was scored.

In June 1922, Rathenau, the foreign minister in the Wirth coalition government, in which the social democrats were a major partner, was murdered by a nationalist gunman. It was the climax in a series of murders by right-wing gangs loosely connected with the army and the police. There had been at least 354 such murders since January 1919, followed by only twenty-four convictions, and these received derisory sentences—the average was four months imprisonment.[10]

After the murder of Rathenau, the KPD was able to force the ADGB union federation, the SPD, and the rump of the USPD (which did not fuse with the SPD until September) to join mass demonstrations for a purge of right-wingers from the army, the civil service, and the courts, for a general amnesty for political prisoners—there were several thousand, overwhelmingly left-wingers—and for suppression of the nationalist gangs. The movement was on such a scale that the Wirth government felt it necessary to introduce legislation conceding these demands, in principle.

The left of the KPD, however, now led by Arkady Maslow and Ruth Fischer, was violently critical of the conduct of the operation by the majority of the party leadership headed by Meyer and Brandler. Most of the left's arguments were worthless—in effect they were variants of the "theory of the offensive"—but one merits discussion. For the left argued that to make demands on the government, or on the SPD leaders without whom the government could not survive, was to reinforce illusions in bourgeois democracy and in the possibility that the SPD and ADGB bureaucrats could really fight the reactionaries.

This argument was wrong on three counts. First, the overwhelming need in the period after the March Madness was to force the KPD membership to accept the united front tactic *in practice,* and the Rathenau affair was a tailor-made opportunity to do this. The *main* danger at that time was ultraleftism, not opportunism.

Second, although the tactic of placing demands on reformist leaders has been frequently misused, indeed at times has become a fetish, it is a necessary aspect of mass agitation by a minority workers' party whose aim is to involve large numbers of workers in action. This was possible at the time of the Rathenau affair, and was indeed achieved on some scale. To call for *mass action* to *compel* a government to take certain measures is not at all the same thing as relying on a government to take measures as a result of resolutions or persuasion, which is the reformist approach. As to raising illusions in bourgeois democracy, any gains made through mass working-class action will raise class consciousness and confidence rather than strengthen parliamentarianism.

Thirdly, although there is very real danger in calling for state action against the right—in this case the nationalist gangs, the overall package, which was necessarily a compromise with the reformists and centrists, was justified *in the given circumstances.*

The short-term results of this and other united front operations, especially in the unions, were favorable to the KPD. Party membership recovered from the low point of mid-1921, reaching 218,000-plus by late 1922. The growth in party influence was claimed to be proportionately greater than the gain in membership. In the same period, the SPD *lost* 47,000 members.

Unfortunately, the experience had negative consequences too. The predominantly right-wing leadership of the KPD became convinced that the party could go on gaining indefinitely, and more or less peacefully, by persistent wooing of the SPD, especially of *its* left wing. The fact that both Meyer and Brandler had supported the March Action, then recoiled violently against adventurism, now led them to give the united front approach a distinctly rightist slant.

Thus at the next party congress, at Leipzig in January 1923, the "workers' government" resolution of the right declared:

> The workers' government is neither the same thing as the proletarian dictatorship, nor is it an attempt to bring this dictatorship about by peaceful parliamentary means; it is an attempt of the working classes to carry out a working-class policy within the framework and, for the time being, with the means of bourgeois democracy, backed by proletarian institutions and mass movements.[11]

This proposition, carried by 122 votes to 81, clearly veered dangerously and impermissibly toward the old social democratic divorce between immediate struggles and the objective of workers' power. By the time it was adopted, the precarious stability of the Weimar Republic was giving way to a new and deeper crisis. The great inflation was well under way and on January 11, 1923, the French army marched into the Ruhr, then the industrial heartland of Germany.

The great inflation began in earnest in June 1922. It took three hundred German marks to buy one U.S. dollar in June. Six months later it took eight thousand. The international value of the mark was halved roughly every six weeks. Prices inside Germany did not rise as fast—but they still rose as never before. The effect on wages was catastrophic. In 1920, German miners, for example, had seen their real wages rise from 60 percent of the 1914 figure to 90 percent. During 1922 they slumped to less than half the 1914 figure.[12]

This was nothing to what was to come. By late summer of 1923, the German currency was effectively worthless. When it was eventually restabilized, on the basis of a new Reichsmark, the value of this was fixed at one to *ten thousand billion* marks!

The galloping inflation of 1922 was largely the product of an attempt by big business to cut back heavily on wages. The hyperinflation that followed, in 1923, was also a weapon of German big business and the new right-wing government under Wilhelm Cuno, a weapon against the Western powers and especially France. Finally the inflation became a self-sustaining monster, uncontrollable without a *decisive* shift in *both* the internal balance of class forces in Germany (either way) *and* in the relationship between Germany and the Western powers.

The Cuno government, which had replaced the Wirth coalition in November 1922, was the most right wing since 1918. Its intentions were to govern without—indeed against—the social democrats and the unions, to scrap the remaining social gains of 1918, especially the eight-hour day, to cut real wages further, and to force the French government and its allies to accept a drastic reduction of reparations payments.

By the Treaty of Versailles, the German state was obliged to pay, in annual installments, "reparations" for war damage, mainly to France and Belgium. The total to be paid, 132 billion gold marks—in other words, marks at their 1914 value, vastly higher than the already heavily depreciated currency of 1919—indicates less the massive size of this burden than does the fact that the "reparations" included the handing over of one quarter of Germany's total coal output.

It was on the coal deliveries that Cuno defaulted, hoping to force a negotiated reduction. The equally right-wing French government, headed by Raymond Poincaré, retaliated by sending its army into the Ruhr in January 1923, supported by Belgian forces, to take the coal itself. Two days later, the German government called for "passive resistance and noncooperation" with the occupying forces. It hoped not only to embarrass the French but also to whip up nationalist hysteria and thus weaken the German workers' resistance to the right. At first it had some success in this.

The KPD responded well. When Cuno demanded a vote of confidence in the Reichstag for his policy and for "national unity," the handful of KPD deputies voted alone against it. The party line was summed up in the slogan "Hit Poincaré on the Ruhr and Cuno on the Spree," meaning in Berlin.

The Comintern organized a campaign of international solidarity. The French Communist Party (PCF), from which Frossard and his friends had just split, organized a vigorous campaign.

> On January 18, 19, and 20, thirty meetings were organized in different quarters of Paris protesting [against] the occupation of the Ruhr. *L'Humanité* published an appeal, from the Comintern and the Profintern to French workers (January 19) declaring that

"Your enemy is at home".... If the government repression is any gauge...the French did their duty. By the end of April, the Santé [prison] was bursting with Communists...syndicalists...and Communist Youth...charged with an impressive array of offenses running from "provocation to crimes against the external and internal security of the state" to "provocation of soldiers with the intention of diverting them from their duties."[13]

This international agitation was a factor weakening the appeal to German workers for "national unity," which had at first been strong. Another factor was the evident collaboration of the industrialists of the Ruhr with the French, whenever it was profitable for them. A third factor, the most important of all, was the onset of hyperinflation in April. Prices began to double weekly, then daily. A massive wave of unofficial strikes, economic strikes as wages became valueless, began in the Ruhr and swept most of Germany in May, June, and early July.

The union leaderships lost control. Factory councils became the effective leading bodies. Already, late in 1922, a KPD-influenced meeting of Berlin factory councils had called on the ADGB leadership to summon a national meeting of councils. When this was refused, predictably, the meeting was called independently by the Berlin councils. The nucleus of a national organization, predominantly influenced by the KPD, was set up.

In the upsurge of spring 1923, this gained much wider influence. Two initiatives were especially important. First the call to set up "proletarian hundreds," effectively a workers' militia based on the workplaces, to resist the right; and secondly the call for "control committees" of the councils plus working-class housewives to take direct action against price rises. By the autumn, there were some eight hundred proletarian hundreds, totaling about sixty thousand workers according to KPD figures. Trotsky later argued that the factory councils could have effectively substituted for soviets; indeed they approximated the soviet form of organization.

The KPD was rapidly growing in influence and numbers, gaining seventy thousand members before June; forms of working-class organization outside the control of the reformist bureaucracies were being created; and there was mass radicalization, a general mood that "things can't go on like this."

In short, there was a revolutionary situation.

But its outcome depended, as always, on leadership. The movement needed a focus, specific objectives that, once won, would carry it forward to struggle for power; and the actual seizure of power had to be organized, the bourgeois state, re-created by the Social Democrats in 1919, had to be destroyed again. All this required from the KPD both firmness and flexibility, "political flair" as Lenin had called it. Clear objectives, but also rapid responses to an ever-shifting situation.

Until the summer, the KPD had not done badly at all, apart from a temporary wobble toward nationalism.[14] True, the party was taken by surprise by the strike wave in May. Nevertheless, the solid united front work that it had done around the factory councils enabled it to catch up, and the orientation it gave to the councils was unquestionably correct. But alone this was insufficient.

The KPD needed not only general political slogans— "Down with Cuno," "For a workers' government" were its main themes—but also specific objectives, specific calls for mass action that would test its influence and the temperature of the movement, and which would sharpen the polarization of workers against the social democratic right.

It appeared to have found one such objective in the Antifascist Day. The far right too was growing, although in most of Germany its weight was still much less than that of the left. But in Bavaria, a right-wing provincial government harassed even the SPD, and the Nazi Party was a growing force, with a good deal of support from sections of the army. In early July, Brandler called for preparation for armed struggle against the fascists and for a national Antifascist Day of aggressive demonstrations on July 29.

Now this was still a united front operation. All workers' organizations were urged to take part, and rightly so. Yet at the same time, it made way for a shift from the defensive (for which the united front was conceived) toward the offensive. For the demonstrations were, in the circumstances, certain to be violent, and the right-wing social democrats were certain to oppose them. Thus the degree of differentiation between left and right in the social democratic ranks could be tested in practice, and so could the willingness of non-party workers to rally to a call for action.

The call for the Antifascist Day was not adventurism. The experience of the Kapp Putsch was fresh in the minds of millions of workers. The Cuno government was visibly failing. A fresh attempt to overthrow the republic from the right appeared a real possibility. "The Cuno government is bankrupt. The internal and external crises have brought it to the verge of catastrophe," wrote Brandler. "We are on the verge of bitter struggles. We must be entirely ready to act."[15]

So far, so good. But the KPD leadership soon began to lose its nerve. The SPD-controlled government of Prussia, Germany's largest province, banned the proposed demonstration. Other provincial governments followed, though not those of Saxony and Thuringia, which were controlled by left social democrats. Brandler found himself opposed in the KPD's leading committee, not only from the right but also from the left—which seems to have opposed all his proposals, good and bad alike, in the spirit of institutionalized factionalism. He consulted the Comintern executive by telegram. The reply, signed by Radek, read: "The Presidium of the International advises abandoning the demonstrations on 29 July.... We fear a trap."[16] The KPD complied.

It was a serious mistake. It had been an excellent opportunity for a practical test of the balance of forces, with minimal risk *and* a chance of moving toward a more serious offensive in the event of success. It had been missed. It was not, in itself, a disastrous error—as events were to show—but it was an ominous sign of the divisions, weaknesses, and lack of self-confidence in the KPD leadership, *and* in the Comintern center.

In the event, this retreat was scarcely noticed at the time. It was masked by mass meetings held in place of demonstrations, and an audience of two hundred thousand was claimed in Berlin. In early August, with hyperinflation reaching its peak, a fresh and even more massive strike wave erupted. This transformed the situation. The delegates of the Berlin factory councils called for an immediate general strike on August 11 to bring down Cuno and establish a workers' government. It paralyzed the capital. Elsewhere the situation was fluid, but the scale of strikes proved sufficient.

Cuno threw in his hand. A new government was formed. Not a workers' government. A "grand coalition" of the SPD with all the "respectable" bourgeois parties. Only the KPD and the Nazis were excluded. Gustav Stresemann, the new chancellor, was a member of the same right-wing party as Cuno, but he saw that Cuno's plan was not feasible. He sought to use the SPD to control the German workers—with four SPD ministers to give his government a "left face"—and he sought to come to terms with the French government with the aid of the British and American ruling classes.

The role of the SPD in this was central and indispensable. Even then, the prospect for the German bourgeoisie looked extremely poor. The historian E. H. Carr, who was exceptionally well informed about German and European politics of this period, wrote: "Few people, inside Germany or outside...had any confidence in the ability of the Stresemann government to weather the storm."[17]

The SPD was deeply split. Although the party had "tolerated" Cuno until the eleventh hour, voting for his measures in the Reichstag or abstaining, its right-wing leadership had increasing difficulty in controlling even its parliamentary fraction. In the vote of confidence for Stresemann's government, 53 of the 171 SPD deputies broke discipline and abstained. The KPD's united front tactic had brought real results.

In Saxony and Thuringia, the left SPD governments ruled with KPD support, despite hostility from the SPD center. These facts are important. They are part of the evidence, of which the mass strikes involving hundreds of thousands of SPD supporters was the most important fact, that by August 1923 the KPD's political *line*, as distinct from the KPD itself, had the support of the great majority of German workers.

Problem: The "workers' government" could not be realized in parliamentary terms. The workers' parties did not have a Reichstag majority. In a number of provinces, they did. The SPD and KPD had, together, a voting majority in these provinces. Nevertheless, the Berlin center was decisive for the time being. The SPD was able to carry its coalition with the boss class on the basis of "practicability" and that it was the "lesser evil." To the majority of workers who supported the SPD, or supported no party, the factory councils did not seem to offer a *government* alternative. There was therefore a lull in struggle. The KPD needed a new orientation.

There is no doubt that this *was* a revolutionary situation, probably more so than in the spring. Numerous observers, from all points of the political compass, testify to this. One will suffice to give the flavor:

> In September and October and November, Germany lived through a profound revolutionary experience.... A million revolutionaries, ready, awaiting the signal to attack; behind them the millions of unemployed, the hungry, the desperate, a people in pain murmuring "Us as well, us as well." The muscles of the crowd were ready, the fists already clasping the Mausers [rifles] that they were going to oppose to the armored cars of the Reichswehr.[18]

What political call was needed? What slogans should the KPD advance?

The KPD continued to call for a workers' government, to call for the SPD to break from the bourgeois parties. Undoubtedly this was correct, so far as it went, but essentially a propaganda slogan. Right and necessary, but quite inadequate in a revolutionary situation. What else? They called for the defense of the state governments controlled by the left SPD and supported by the KPD. This was right enough, in the circumstances, a way to win the majority of workers to action. And this defensive action could then go on to the offensive—though only on the basis that it was generalized throughout Germany, spread to the Ruhr and to Prussia.

Now let us look back to the Comintern center. When Brandler's telegram asking for advice about the Antifascist Day reached Moscow, *all* the influential Russian leaders apart from Lenin, who was incapacitated, were on holiday. Radek was obliged to telegraph them. The answers—Zinoviev and Bukharin said the Antifascist Day should go ahead; Stalin said back down, Trotsky, "don't know"—were much less significant than the fact that all of them, Trotsky included, were so preoccupied with Russian matters that they had failed to take seriously the developing revolutionary situation in Germany.

The fall of Cuno woke them up. For a brief period, the Russian leadership, for the last time, was united in favor of an attempt by a major communist party to seize power. Even Stalin was temporarily moved. "The revolution in Germany is the most important event of our time," he wrote. "The victory of the German Revolution will be still more important for the proletariat of Europe and America than was the Russian Revolution of six years ago. The victory of the German Revolution will transfer the center of world revolution from Moscow to Berlin."[19] But the trumpet sounded an uncertain note. The leaders of the German KPD, although prodded from Moscow, had no real faith in their ability to conduct a successful defense of Saxony and Thuringia and then go over to the offensive. All their mistakes of the past five years: the Spartakus rising, the abstentionism in the first days of the Kapp Putsch, the March Action, had been "leftist" errors. Now they had learned the lesson well, too well. Faced with a real revolutionary situation, they shrank back.

True enough, they committed themselves to an insurrection, but in fear and trembling rather than boldness and resolution. They undertook technical preparations. Indeed, they so overestimated the need for practical and military preparations that they underplayed the political preparations, the need for mass agitation, for continuing contact with the mass of the working class.

The plan, a hodgepodge compromise among the German, Russian, and Comintern leaderships, was for the KPD to enter the Saxon and Thuringian governments (the left SPD leaders were eager to have them in as "left cover"), then arm the workers from the provincial arsenals. When, inevitably, the central government sent in the Reichswehr, they would resist and launch an all-German insurrection through the proletarian hundreds.

But there were key weaknesses in this. First, those on the left of the SPD were not ready for civil war. They dragged their feet and dragged the KPD behind them. Secondly, the technical and political maneuvers so preoccupied the KPD that the political needs of the situation—mass agitation, support and leadership of partial struggles, a raising of the temperature back to August levels—were relatively neglected.

On October 20, the Reichswehr marched into Saxony. The SPD majority in the Saxon government refused to back armed resistance or the call for a national general strike. The KPD leadership buckled. The national insurrection, planned for October 22, was called off by the party. This message did not reach Hamburg, however, where an isolated rising took place and, being isolated, was inevitably crushed.

Thus the German October ended in a victory for Stresemann and the bourgeoisie. And this proved decisive for the fate of the Comintern.

It was not the *decisive* defeat in Germany itself, although it was the most serious setback since 1918. The "grand coalition" still rested on the SPD, in other words on the labor bureaucracies. The German workers' movement was weakened but intact. The KPD, although outlawed for a time, was not crushed. Indeed, in 1924, it appeared to have strengthened its position with respect to the SPD. In the general election of May 1924, the first since 1920, the KPD polled 3,693,300 votes to the SPD's 6,008,900, winning 62 deputies to the SPD's 99. In purely electoral terms, this was an advance, and was claimed as such by the "left" KPD leaders who had ousted Brandler. Before the election, the KPD had had only 14 deputies.

(The Nazis received 1,918,300 votes, half as many as the KPD, which proves that the Nazi threat grew *after* the failure of 1923 and, in part, as a result of it—and not at all when the revolutionary tide was running.)

But for the KPD, this was, in fact, not an advance at all, but a decline. As Trotsky argued in June 1924:

> In the last parliamentary election, the Communist Party polled 3,700,000 votes. That, of course, is a very fine nucleus of the proletariat. But the figure has to be evaluated dynamically. There can be no doubt that in August–October of last year, the Communist Party could have polled an incomparably greater number of votes. On the other hand, there is much to suggest that had the elections taken place two or three months later, the Communist Party's vote would have been smaller. This means, in other words, that the party's influence is now on the decline. *It would be absurd to shut one's eyes to this: revolutionary politics are not the politics of the ostrich....*
> After the defeat of 1905 [in Russia], we needed seven years before the movement, stimulated by the Lena events, began once again to turn upwards.... The German proletariat suffered last year a very big defeat. It will need a definite and considerable interval of time in order to digest this defeat, master its lessons, and recover from it, gathering strength once more; and the Communist Party will be able to ensure the victory of the proletariat only if it, too, fully and completely masters the lessons of last year's experience.
> How much time will be needed for these processes? Five years? Twelve years? No precise answer can be given.... But at

the present moment, what we observe are phenomena of ebb tide and not of floodtide, and our tactics should, of course, conform to this situation."[20]

The actual outcome for the KPD was a wholly inappropriate shift to the left, in part to ultraleft stupidities. This was followed, in 1925, by an overcorrection rightward. The party remained a force in the working class, although a minority compared to the SPD. It was to have one more big chance, and only one, in 1930–32. But by that time, it had become a tool of the Comintern, which had itself become purely a tool of Russian foreign policy.

The reaction in Russia

"If we do not close our eyes to reality we must admit that, at the present time, the proletarian policy of the party is not determined by the character of its membership, but by the enormous undivided prestige enjoyed by the small group which might be called the Old Guard of the party. A slight conflict within this group will be enough, if not to destroy this prestige, to weaken the group to such a degree as to rob it of its power to determine policy."
Lenin, Letter to the Central Committee, March 1922

IT WAS in Russia that October 1923 was decisive. The sick, bureaucratized workers' state was shifted sharply rightward. The bureaucracy began to acquire its own collective consciousness, defined, as always, *against* that of other groups. In October 1923, even Stalin, already emerging as the leader of the bureaucracy, had been moved to write: "The revolution approaching in Germany is the most important international event of our time."

In bureaucratic circles, this mood rapidly evaporated with the defeat. We need to look at these circles more closely. At the eleventh congress of the Russian Communist Party in March–April 1922, the last at which Lenin was able to participate, he said in his opening speech:

> If we take Moscow with its 4,700 communists in responsible positions, and if we take that huge bureaucratic machine, that gigantic heap, we must ask: who is directing whom? I very much doubt whether it can truthfully be said that the communists are directing that heap. To tell the truth, they are not directing, they are being directed.... Will the responsible

communists of the RSFSR and of the Russian Communist Party realize that they cannot administer; that they only imagine that they are directing, but are, actually, being directed?[21]

The vast majority of these bureaucrats were political "radishes": they had a thin red skin, all white inside. They were of the Russian middle classes, reincarnated as Soviet officials. How did this come about? Lenin's answer is revealing: "Their culture is miserable, insignificant, but it is still at a higher level than ours. Miserable and low as it is, it is higher than that of our responsible communist administrators, for the latter lack administrative ability."[22]

This is revealing because it took for granted that the commune state, the "not quite a state" of Lenin's *State and Revolution*, the state of "every cook can govern," no longer existed. Control of the state was no longer a question of workers' power but of the cultural level of the communists with respect to that of the "radishes"!

But this is substitutionism to the furthest degree: party control of the state substituting for the workers. And Lenin knew it. Far too profound a Marxist to fail to face the reality, he sought palliatives to minimize the evil until help could come from outside, from the working classes of the fully industrialized countries, from workers capable of full self-emancipation and self-rule. The last months of Lenin's conscious life, half-paralyzed as he was, were devoted to an increasingly desperate struggle against the bureaucracy in the state and in the party. Hence his proposal that Stalin be removed from the post of party general secretary. But it was a struggle from the top, inevitably so in the circumstances, and "the enormous undivided prestige" of the old guard could not for long continue to preserve a "proletarian policy" without a real shift in the international balance of class forces.

The German October was such a shift—but in the wrong direction. It was followed, after Lenin's death, by the campaigns against Trotsky. It was followed by the "Lenin levy"— the mass recruitment into the party of people who had *not* joined in the years of revolution and civil war, who had not joined through class struggle, and who could, joining now, for the most part be counted upon to support those who controlled patronage, promotion, and, increasingly, privilege. It was followed finally by the bureaucracy's "declaration of independence," the new ideology of "socialism in one country."

As late as May 1924, Stalin himself had repeated the orthodox Marxist position:

> The principal task of socialism—the organization of socialist production—has still to be fulfilled. Can this task be fulfilled, can the final victory of socialism be achieved, in one country, without the joint efforts of the proletarians in several advanced countries? No it cannot...for the organization of socialist production, the efforts of one country, particularly of a peasant country like Russia, are insufficient; for that the efforts of the proletarians of several advanced countries are required.[23]

But with the defeat in Germany in October 1923, continued adherence to the goal of international socialist revolution had few attractions. For the consolidating and increasingly privileged bureaucracy, the main consideration was peace at any price, short of their own displacement by internal or external reaction. Continued internationalist "adventures" might lead to revolutionary crises and perhaps renewed imperialist interventions against the USSR.

This is the basic truth, but it must not be viewed in too simplistic a way. "Privilege" was highly relative—nothing like the enormous differences in living standards that exist between ordinary workers and the top bureaucrats in the USSR today. But about 20 percent of the urban working class was unemployed. A secure office job was "privilege." The prospect of such a position through loyal service to "the Party," meaning the party machine, was a powerful incentive to conformity. And this conservative trend in the working class was reinforced by the emergence, out of the ranks of the peasant majority, of a layer of relatively better-off farmers. These were the social forces on which Stalin's party machine was to be built.

"Socialism in one country" fitted well with the needs and aspirations of the newly emerging bureaucracy. It meant focusing on a *national* arena that they could aspire to control, rather than on an international class struggle that they could not. At the same time, it was a banner around which they could group. As Trotsky put it, socialism in one country "expressed unmistakably the mood of the bureaucracy. When speaking of the victory of socialism, they meant their own victory."[24]

But this was as yet only the start of the battle. In 1923–24, the Russian bureaucracy was feeling only the first stirrings of political consciousness as an independent social force. Many bitter political and economic struggles had yet to be fought before it could rule both party and state, politically and economically, with national development as its central and controlling aim.

At the end of 1923, Stalin's party machine was still far from being able to dictate to the major communist parties. It still had to deal circumspectly with revolutionary tendencies at home and abroad. It needed allies with better revolutionary credentials than its own, and it needed time to subvert the still powerful traditions of the first four congresses of the Comintern. Therefore, in the immediate aftermath of the German October, it put its weight behind Zinoviev's "leftism" so as better to eliminate the genuine article, the revolutionary internationalism represented by Trotsky.

By December 1924, the profession of belief in "socialism in one country," in other words in Russia, had become the test of party loyalty and reliability. Those so rash as to adhere to the position that even Stalin had upheld a few short months earlier were beyond the pale.

The impact of this on the Comintern was profound. The Comintern was still needed. Russia was still economically and militarily weak. Its rulers needed all the support from abroad that they could get. But, inevitably now, the Comintern became more and more dominated by considerations, not of international socialist revolution, but of Russian foreign policy. And that required its transformation into an obedient instrument of Moscow and, ultimately, a *conservative* force. The process took a long time to complete. But 1923 marked the turning point.

FIVE

LEFT OSCILLATION, RIGHT TURN
1924–1928

"The policy of the most important communist parties, attuned to the fifth congress, soon revealed its complete inefficacy. The mistakes of pseudo-"leftism," which hampered the development of the communist parties, gave an impetus to a new empirical zigzag: namely to an accelerated sliding down to the right.... The adventurist leftism gave way to an open opportunism of the right centrist type."

Trotsky, *Strategy and Tactics in the Imperialist Epoch*

THE IMMEDIATE response of the Comintern leadership to the failure of the German October was to proclaim the correctness of its own role at every stage, to sacrifice scapegoats, and to proclaim that there was a *continuing* revolutionary situation in Germany. "The basic appraisal of the German situation given by the Comintern executive last September remains in essentials unchanged," declared the executive in January 1924. "The character of the phase in the struggle and the chief tasks of the party are the same. The KPD must not strike from the agenda the question of insurrection and seizure of power."[1]

It was a case, as Trotsky sourly remarked, of "accepting the backside for the face of the revolution after the latter had already turned its rear"[2]—and it was typical of the short-lived "left oscillation." Rhetoric, bluff, fantasy, and, above all, lack of honest accounting were its hallmarks. Along with this went a rather shame-faced ultraleftism, but this was not universally applied: the British, U.S., Chinese, and Yugoslav communist parties were unaffected.

And there were changes in the party leaderships. In Germany, the lefts—Arkady Maslow, Ruth Fischer, and their supporters—took over the KPD, which regained legal status in March 1924. In Poland, where there had been a general strike in November 1923 and a local insurrection in Krakow, the "rightist" leadership of Adolf Warski, Henryk Walecki, and Wera Kostryewa was replaced by the left-wingers Domski, Zofia Unslicht, and Lenski. In France, Rosmer, Monatte, and Souvarine were eliminated, and Zinoviev's protegés Albert Treint and Suzanne Girault were installed. In Sweden, the rightist Seth Hoeglund was replaced by Karl Kilbom. But these changes were by no means politically identical. This was Zinoviev's Comintern, not yet Stalin's. The "Troika" of Zinoviev, Stalin, and Kamenev had defeated the left opposition at the thirteenth conference of the Communist Party of the Soviet Union (CPSU) in January 1924 and its thirteenth congress in May. They were now vigorously promoting a cult of "Leninism"—by which was meant opposition to the political line pursued by Trotsky—and great efforts were made, successfully, to secure endorsement of this from foreign communist parties. The Comintern was now Zinoviev's fiefdom. But there was still some debate in the various communist parties. The new left leaders had varying degrees of genuine support in their parties. They were not all simply creatures of Moscow. Significantly, most of them were soon in conflict with the Comintern executive.

Thus the Maslow-Fischer group had the overwhelming majority at the Frankfurt congress of the KPD in April 1924 and brushed aside the attempt of the Comintern representative, Manuilsky, to moderate their victory by including some representatives of the old leadership in the new one. In Sweden, Kilbom undoubtedly had majority support and would have ousted Hoeglund even without Comintern support. In Poland and France, however, matters were somewhat different.

> In the autumn of 1923, the central committees of the Polish, French, and German parties protested, in one form or another, to the central committee of the Soviet party against the violence of the attacks on Trotsky.... This incident had serious consequences. Stalin never forgot or forgave this protest. Zinoviev, who was then president of the International, viewed it as a vote of no confidence in himself.[3]

The attack on "the three Ws" in the Polish party had more to do with their reluctance to condemn Trotsky than with their real waverings in November 1923. Those who replaced them had real support but not a majority—they owed their victory to the intervention by the Comintern executive. So, still more, did Treint and Girault in France. Thus, an evil precedent was created by Zinoviev. He and his supporters were soon to fall victim to it themselves.

Politically, the period of the "left oscillation" is significant for the abandonment of the united front tactic in practice—although, characteristically, it was retained in words; for the first appearance of the notorious doctrine of "social fascism" and for "Bolshevization."

"Bolshevization" was the watchword of the fifth congress of the Comintern in June–July 1924. It was the precise counterpart to the cult of the dead Lenin in the USSR and its actual content was the same: unqualified submission to the Troika as the supposed guardians of Leninist orthodoxy and hostility to all critical voices, above all to Trotsky. Naturally this "Leninism" had nothing in common with the spirit of Lenin's own politics. He himself had written, some years earlier, of the fate of great revolutionaries: "After their deaths, attempts are made to convert them into harmless icons, to canonize them so to say, and to hallow their *names*...whilst at the same time robbing the revolutionary theory of its *substance*, blunting its revolutionary edge and vulgarizing it."[4] This is an exact description of the function of "Leninism" and its Comintern counterpart "Bolshevization" in this period.

On the united front tactic, the fifth world congress made a formally correct declaration.[5] After all, the Troika was wrapping itself in the mantle of Lenin and Lenin's pronouncements on the matter were all too recent and well known. But the whole emphasis of Zinoviev's speech on orientation and tactics was in the other direction. "Only from below" was the substance of Zinoviev's line, meaning that united front action should be proposed only to the rank and file of other parties and workers' organizations, not to their leaderships.

Now there *are* circumstances in which the united front is clearly inappropriate, a wrong tactic. One such case was in Russia in September–October 1917, in the weeks before the insurrection. Then, a united front approach by the Bolsheviks to the Mensheviks and the right wing of the Socialist Revolutionary Party would have meant stepping back from the struggle for power. Again, in circumstances where the revolutionary left is extremely weak the united front tactic is also wrong—or irrelevant. A united front means *united in action* and is meaningless if the revolutionaries have no real forces to commit to such action.

If the united front tactic is judged inappropriate, then it is politically necessary to say so. The whole thrust of the political line given at the fifth congress of the Comintern was that the *offensive* was the order of the day in a number of countries, especially Germany. This was grotesquely wrong, but if it had been true, then the united front tactic—which, remember, is a *defensive* tactic—should have been seen by the congress as at least secondary and, in particular cases, definitely wrong.

But this was not done. Instead the line of the united front "only from below" was proclaimed. It was nonsense. The essence of the united front tactic is that the appeal for united action is made to the *leadership* of another workers' organization as well as the rank and file, although, of course, everything depends on the response of the rank and file. Unity in action will then prove to the rank and file of that organization that revolutionary politics are superior to that of their own leadership. To make the appeal for united action *only* to the rank and file is not a united front at all—it is merely an appeal to individuals to work with or join the party, an appeal that revolutionaries should make in all circumstances anyway.

Any honest communist party leadership who believed, however mistakenly, in the call for the offensive put forward by the Fifth World Congress would have argued this case. Some did. Bordiga, for the Italians, argued against the united front in principle. Domski, for the Poles, argued against it in practice. But the self-deceiving, shamefaced position put forward by Zinoviev and his supporters carried the day.

The immediate consequences of this were, in fact, fairly unimportant—but the "only from below" line was to be revived, with truly disastrous consequences, in 1929–33.

So too with "social fascism." To start with a genuine principled and incorrigible ultraleft, Bordiga said at the fifth congress:

"Fascism fundamentally merely repeats the old game of the bourgeois left parties, i.e., it appeals to the proletariat for civil peace. It attempts to achieve this aim by forming trade unions of industrial and agricultural workers, which it then leads into practical collaboration with the employers' organizations."[6] What then is the difference between fascism and social democracy? None at all, on this analysis. This is manifest nonsense. The *essential* distinctive characteristic of fascism is that it seeks to *smash* all autonomous workers' organizations, revolutionary and reformist alike, to atomize the working class and so make it politically impotent. This was already happening in Italy in 1924, as Bordiga was speaking. Social democracy, on the other hand, rests upon, parasitizes if you will, genuine workers' organizations. Without them it has no basis at all.

The *class* basis of fascism is *fundamentally* different from that of social democracy. Like revolutionary socialists, the fascists can win a truly *mass* base only in conditions of deep social crisis. But whereas revolutionary socialists depend upon the *organized* working class or on workers fighting to achieve organization, whose collective strength gives these workers the ability to overthrow capitalism and build a new society, the fascists depend upon the petty bourgeoisie and the unorganized and "lumpen" section of the working class. Driven to extremes of insecurity as victims of the crisis, and without their own organizations to defend them, they can be easy recruits to fascism, which offers them the false solidarity of prejudice and paramilitary violence in a time of profound social crisis.

Unlike the social democrats, the fascists have no commitment to bourgeois democracy. Unlike revolutionary socialists they *are* committed to maintain the dictatorship of capital—though since part of their support is from victims of capitalism this involves the liquidation of their "lumpen" working-class wing if they come to power, as Hitler liquidated the Röhm-Strasser wing of the Nazi Party in 1934.

The Fifth World Congress, however, gave countenance to Bordiga's idiocies by enshrining the proposition that "Fascism and social democracy are two edges of the same weapon of the dictatorship of large-scale capital."[7] Stalin's notorious aphorism, "Social democracy and fascism are not antipodes but

twins," belongs to this period. Again the immediate consequences were unimportant but the revival of these notions in
1929–33 was to be catastrophic. Fascism and social democracy
are not two edges of the same weapon. They are *alternative*
supports for capitalism.

The practical outcome of the "left oscillation" was the removal from positions of leadership in the Comintern, and, in
some important communist parties, of independent-minded
people both of the "right" and of the "left" (in communist
terms). Some of these people were clearly in the wrong and
were moving toward social democracy; others were, in varying
degrees, correct in their criticisms. This was a long step toward
the situation against which Lenin had warned Bukharin and
Zinoviev some years earlier: "If you drive away all not particularly amenable but intelligent people and leave yourselves only
obedient fools, you will *surely* destroy the party."[8]

It was also the cause of some tragedies. In December 1924,
the weak Estonian Communist Party, encouraged by Zinoviev,
who was badly in need of a success, launched a coup d'état.
"The insurgents had a few initial successes at Reval, the capital, owing to the advantage of surprise. But after only a few
hours, everything was over. It was a classic example of a hope-
less putsch. The persecutions naturally were intensified after its
failure; and the rising itself provided a suitable occasion to institute a military dictatorship."[9]

Unlike the Reval putsch, the Bulgarian "Guy Fawkes plot"
of April 1925 was not a Comintern initiative, but undoubtedly
owed something to the atmosphere of "leftism" that Zinoviev
had encouraged. The plan of the operation, which was organized by the military organization of the Bulgarian Communist
Party, without the knowledge of the party's leadership-in-exile,
was to blow up Sofia Cathedral at a time when the king, government, and army chiefs were attending the funeral of a murdered general.

> Official Bulgaria assembled *en masse* for the funeral. A bomb
> exploded, killing more than 100 persons and wounding 300,
> though all the members of the government miraculously es-
> caped.... Two leading members of the military organization of
> the Bulgarian Communist Party, Yankov and Minkov, were
> killed resisting arrest. Hundreds of communists were arrested;

confessions were obtained under torture, and many of those arrested were executed, with or without trial.[10]

The Comintern executive denied responsibility, which was the formal truth, and stated the orthodox Marxist case against individual terrorism. The Bulgarian Communist Party was temporarily destroyed in the ensuing repression.

The short-lived oscillation to the left was ended at the fifth plenum of the Comintern executive in March 1925. It was belatedly discovered that "in the center of Europe, in Germany, the period of revolutionary upsurge has already ended."[11] The conclusion drawn was that it was necessary to shift the emphasis back to the united front tactic. "Only from below" and "social fascism" were soon quietly dropped. "Bolshevization" was not. It was emphasized more than ever, and its stance against Trotsky and his supporters became more and more blatant. The shift rightward—correct in itself, if sixteen months too late—soon developed into out-and-out opportunism.

As Trotsky wrote later:

> A cat burned by hot milk shies away from cold water. The "left" central committees of a number of parties were deposed as violently as they had been constituted prior to the fifth congress. The adventurist leftism gave way to an open opportunism of the right-centrist type.
>
> To understand the character and tempo of this organizational rightward swing, it must be recalled that Stalin, the director of this turn, appraised the passing of party leadership to Maslow, Ruth Fischer, Treint, Susanne Girault, and others, back in 1924, as the expression of the Bolshevization of the parties....
>
> But ten months later the genuine "Bolsheviks" and "revolutionary leaders" were declared social democrats and renegades, ousted from leadership and driven out of the parties.[12]

Soon their patron, Zinoviev, was to go too. For the rightward shift in Russia, the growing self-confidence of the bureaucracy with its new slogan of "socialism in one country," led to the breakup of the Troika and the passing of Zinoviev, and then Kamenev, into opposition. Stalin's star was rising.

Zinoviev's period of dominance in the Comintern had been a fiasco. "Leftist" and pseudo-leftist adventures had been combined, as we shall see, with grossly opportunist adventures. Yet, with all his weaknesses and vacillations, there were certain limits beyond which Zinoviev would not go. A Bolshevik since

1903, a member of the Bolshevik central committee since 1907, Lenin's closest collaborator in the early years, he had absorbed too much of Lenin's internationalism to be a suitable instrument of the increasingly nationalistic bureaucratic dictatorship. Although not formally deposed until 1926, Zinoviev lost influence after the fifth plenum of the Comintern executive in early 1925. Stalin was now the leader, though still only the "first among equals" of the newly self-conscious bureaucratic chiefs.

Stalin was a newcomer to the Comintern. "In the days when the Comintern seemed a living organism and engaged the constant and anxious attention of Lenin, Trotsky, and Zinoviev, he [Stalin] remained apparently indifferent to it. He turned to it only in 1924 when it...had become a bureaucratic machine capable of impeding or furthering Soviet policy or his own political designs."[13]

For Stalin, the Comintern was essentially an instrument of Russian foreign policy. However, this could not be openly avowed, nor could Stalin yet run it himself or through puppet nominees. He needed a prominent "old Bolshevik," with some genuine qualifications, who was wholly convinced of the need for a rightist orientation. Nikolai Bukharin was that man. The period of the right turn was the period of Bukharin's Comintern.

Bukharin was a doctrinaire, in the literal sense of the word. Lenin had written of him, in his "testament" just before his death, that Bukharin's "theoretical views can only with the very gravest doubts be regarded as fully Marxist, for there is something scholastic in him (he has never learned, and I think never fully understood, the dialectic)."[14] Bukharin had been a consistent ultraleft in the first years after the Russian Revolution. Now he was, equally consistently and equally mechanically, rightist in his views on the situation inside Russia and internationally. Under his regime, the Comintern underwent a further and qualitative degeneration.

These were the years of the "right-center bloc" in the USSR, the alliance between Stalin and Bukharin, the years of "growing into socialism"—in one country, of course—"at a snail's pace," the years of banking on the peasantry for slow economic growth—"enrich yourselves" was the party's message to them (all those quoted expressions are Bukharin's), the years in which planned industrialization was rejected as "adventurism."

The corresponding policies in the Comintern were those of making alliances with "left" union bureaucrats, "left" labor politicians, and bourgeois and petty-bourgeois nationalists.

"Petty-bourgeois 'allies'"

"Thanks to its privileged position and conservative habits of thinking, the soviet bureaucracy...is far more inclined to trust in the 'revolutionary' Kuomintang, the 'left' bureaucracy of the British trade unions, petty-bourgeois 'friends of the Soviet Union,' and liberal and radical pacifists than in the independent revolutionary initiative of the proletariat."

Trotsky, "The International Left Opposition"

THE ROOTS of the right turn lay in the period of the "left oscillation," not merely by way of reaction against it, but also because the bureaucratic adventurism that characterized Zinoviev's regime in the Comintern contained within it seeds of gross opportunism.

Back in the autumn of 1923, a meeting of delegates allegedly representing peasant organizations in forty countries set up an "International Peasant Council" in Moscow. This shadowy body was described by the Fifth World Congress as the "Peasant International" (Krestintern). Six million supporters were claimed for it, and it was evidently seen as a hook with which important catches could be made. Negotiations were opened with the leaders of the exiled Bulgarian Peasants Union. They were promised subsidies if they would join the Krestintern. The wily Bulgars took the money (allegedly twenty million dinars) and slipped away.[15]

Their success may have encouraged Stephan Radich, leader of the Croat Peasant Party. He came to Moscow in 1924, and actually affiliated his party to the Krestintern. Having thus alarmed the Yugoslav government, he came to terms with it and took his party into a coalition government: "En route from green Zagreb, he thought it advisable to show himself in Red Moscow in order to strengthen his chances of becoming a minister in White Belgrade," noted Trotsky.[16]

Little more was heard of the Krestintern, although, as we shall see, it survived long enough to play a minor role in the

Comintern's disastrous intervention in the Chinese revolution of 1925–27.

Then there was the comic interlude of the Federated Farmer-Labor Party. "In the United States, the small farmers have founded a Farmer-Labor Party, which is becoming ever more radical, drawing closer to the communists, and becoming permeated with the idea of the creation of a workers' and peasants' government in the United States," it was claimed at the Fifth World Congress.[17]

What lay behind this fantasy was a small Labor Party movement centered on the leftish leaders of the Chicago Federation of Labor (the local leadership of the AFL). They had their own Farmer-Labor party (the "farmer" being added to the title to attract votes, for this was a purely electoral affair) and were seeking to broaden it by a conference in Chicago in July 1923.

The American communist party, then called the Workers Party, set out to capture this conference, and so, it imagined, a growing movement. The party was small; it claimed some fourteen thousand members, most of them recent immigrants, the majority not speaking English, and it had until very recently been wildly ultraleft. Now, under the guidance of a Hungarian Comintern official called Pogany (Pepper in the United States), it proposed to break into big-time electoral politics with the presidential election of 1924, via a front party.

> Several hundred delegates, claiming to represent some 600,000 workers and farmers came to Chicago for the Farmer-Labor convention…. Only ten delegates were officially allotted to the Workers Party…but the communists had other ways of getting in. Dozens attended as delegates from local trade unions. Others managed to represent such organizations as the Lithuanian Workers Literature Society, the Rumanian Progressive Club, the United Workingmen Singers, and so on.[18]

The genuine Farmer-Labor Party supporters did not represent a great deal in the American working class, but they represented something—their presidential candidate had polled a quarter of a million votes in 1920. The Workers Party represented practically nothing, but it had the delegates and so was able to take over the convention. The genuine Farmer-Labor supporters walked out. Workers Party nominees for president and vice president of the United States were duly adopted. The party's leaders were jubilant. The Workers Party "assumed the position of leadership and the first mass party of the American workers—the Federated Farmer-Labor Party—was formed."[19]

What the Workers Party had actually "assumed the position of leadership" of was a shell—a reformist shell, for the program actually adopted was practically identical to that of the old Farmer-Labor Party, and a shell so fragile that it completely disintegrated within a year, leaving the Workers Party rather weaker than before.

These foolish opportunist schemes took place under the regime of the "left oscillation." The much more serious Polish "May Error" occurred when the "right turn" was already fully in motion.

The policies of the ultraleft leadership installed in 1924 had seriously weakened the Polish Communist Party. It should be noted that, throughout the period when it was a genuine workers' party, 1919–38, the Polish Communist Party was an illegal organization, though possibilities for semi-legal activity varied greatly. It usually worked through legal "cover" organizations.

> If, in 1923, the party did not show enough revolutionary vigor, its policy during the years 1924 and 1925 was marked by a false excess of that vigor. This was all the more harmful because after the crisis of November 1923 the objective possibilities of revolutionary action had decreased. During the period the Polish Communist Party rejected the united front tactic completely and dispersed its efforts in futile adventures. The result? It lost its influence and cut itself off from the working masses.
>
> It is worth recalling that, at the beginning of 1924, in local elections, the Polish Communist Party was still stronger than the Socialist Party. This success, however, was no more than a delayed echo of the radicalization of the masses which had taken place in 1923 and did not foreshadow the rise of a new revolutionary wave [exactly as in Germany]. In the following year, the Communist Party's influence declined drastically.[20]

For these reasons, and still more because Domski and Zofia Unslicht were honest and conscientious supporters of Zinoviev, they were ousted. Warski and his friends, who had meanwhile made the required denunciation of Trotsky, were reinstated as the leadership in December 1925. There was one significant change. Lenski broke with his former associates, preferring to declare unqualified support for the CPSU (in fact, for Stalin), and was henceforth Stalin's man in Poland—the prototype for Thälmann in Germany, Thorez in France, Browder in the United States, Pollitt in Britain, and the rest. He was included in the new leadership, which steered the party sharply to the right.

On May 12, 1926, Joseph Pilsudski, who had been commander-in-chief of the Polish army when it defeated the Red Army in 1920, launched a coup d'état against Poland's right-wing bourgeois democratic government, which was headed by the Peasant Party leader Witos. The Polish Communist Party *supported* the coup, which was successful and created a military dictatorship that the Comintern was soon to call "Pilsudski's fascist regime"!

How was this lunacy possible? Because the Polish Socialist Party supported Pilsudski, who had once been one of its members and leader of its "revolutionary fraction"—in other words its terrorist wing—in 1905–06, and the united front policy was now interpreted as meaning that the Polish Communist Party tailed the Socialist Party. That and the absurd notion, a product of the anti-Trotsky campaigns, that the revolution in Poland had to be a *bourgeois* revolution and therefore Pilsudski was the Polish Cromwell.

> The Comintern was just then busy eradicating the Trotskyist and Zinovievist heresies. The distinctive marks of these heresies were defined as "ultraleft" and negative attitudes toward "alliances with the middle strata," a fundamental unwillingness to make such alliances and an unwillingness to recognize that bourgeois revolution, especially in the underdeveloped countries, formed a separate stage of the historical development, in which the bourgeoisie played a progressive and even revolutionary role.
>
> The Comintern was as if seized with an obsessional cult of "alliances." Any sign of skepticism with regard to this cult was stigmatized as Trotskyism. The cult of alliances served a double purpose: within the Soviet Union it justified the rightist line of Bukharin and Stalin; internationally it justified Soviet policy in China, which subordinated the Chinese Communist Party to the Kuomintang and placed it under Chiang Kai-shek's orders.[21]

Of course all this garbage had to be junked very quickly in the case of Poland. Pilsudski, a reliable ally of French imperialism, was bitterly hostile to the USSR and his regime persecuted the workers' organizations, particularly the Polish Communist Party, far more viciously and effectively than Witos had ever done.

The British general strike

"Zinoviev gave us to understand that he counted on the revolution finding an entrance, not through the narrow gateway of the British Communist Party, but through the broad portals of the trade unions. The struggle to win the masses organized in the trade unions by the Communist Party was replaced by the hope for the swiftest possible utilization of the ready-made apparatus of the trade unions for the purpose of revolution. Out of this false position sprang the later policy of the Anglo-Russian Committee..."

Trotsky, "What We Gave and What We Got:
Balance Sheet of the Anglo-Russian Committee"

THAT SAME May 1926 saw the British general strike. The story will no doubt be familiar to most readers.[22] As has been noted, the British Communist Party was unaffected by the "left oscillation." In 1924, the central thrust of its activity was united front work in the unions, focused around the National Minority Movement. This essentially correct work was given a rightist twist with the formation of the Anglo-Soviet Trade Union Committee in April 1925—about which the Comintern was extraordinarily enthusiastic.

"The change in sentiment among the working masses and the majority of the organized working class in England is expressed organizationally in the creation of the Anglo-Russian unity committee," declared the sixth plenum of the Comintern executive in March 1926. "The Anglo-Russian committee, whose foundation was greeted joyfully by the masses, marks a new stage in the history of the international trade union movement.... It demonstrates the practical possibility of creating a unified International, and of a common struggle of workers of different political tendencies against reaction, fascism, and the capitalist offensive."[23]

What it in fact demonstrated was that the temporarily dominant left-reformist bureaucrats on the British TUC General Council found it useful to acquire some "left" cover, protection from communist party criticism at practically no cost. In the period from July 1925 to May 1926, the British government was coldly and carefully preparing to break the power of the miners' union. In this same period, the left trade union leaders, heroes of the Anglo-Soviet Trade Union Committee, bemused their followers

LEFT OSCILLATION, RIGHT TURN   119

with leftist rhetoric, made *no* preparations for the inevitable conflict with the government and covered up for the right. Within two months of the sixth plenum, which was so vocal in their praise, they had joined with the right to sell out the general strike.

These left officials were by no means unknown to the leaders of the British Communist Party. They were, typically, men who had been involved in the pre-1914 syndicalist and amalgamationist movements, had moved up various union machines and become very much part of the union establishment, constituting its left face. A number of them had even joined the Communist Party in 1920 or 1921 but had left again as soon as the party began to put pressure on them to act as disciplined party members. At best, they could only be vacillating and unreliable allies. At least some of the Communist Party leaders understood this well enough. "It would be suicidal policy, however, for the Communist Party and the Minority Movement to place too much reliance on what we have called the official left wing," declared the party's monthly journal in September 1924.[24] The emphasis had to be on "the formation of workplace committees [as] a necessary means of counteracting the bureaucracy."

This emphasis shifted sharply when the Anglo-Soviet committee was set up, ostensibly "to promote the cause of unity in the international trade union movement" as a step toward "international unity of the workers of all countries" and "an unbreakable pledge of peace and economic security."[25] The agreement with the Russian unions was endorsed *unanimously* by the British TUC that September. The British Communist Party then proceeded to adopt the "suicidal" policy. Of course there were "native" opportunist tendencies in the party leadership that were only too glad to adapt to the TUC's fake left, but it was the Comintern and Russian leaders who ensured that the opportunist line was consistently pursued.

The thinking of the Russian leaders at this time was dominated by the idea that whereas the British Communist Party was small and weak, the TUC was a *power* in Britain, a power that could be exerted in the interests of the USSR. The job of the Communist Party was therefore to encourage the TUC, not to upset it by "premature" criticism.

What was criminal about this episode was not the Anglo-Soviet committee itself, which was possibly justified as a temporary maneuver to weaken the Amsterdam International; it was the deliberate creation of illusions in the TUC "lefts" and the political *paralysis* imposed upon the British Communist Party by the Comintern. During the nine-month "truce" between government and unions leading up to May 1926, it was essential for the Communist Party to criticize, constantly, concretely, and clearly, the inactivity of the left trade union leaders in the face of the government preparations for a showdown, to warn of impending disaster, to exert all its efforts to develop rank-and-file preparation *independently* of the union bureaucracies, "left" as well as right. Instead it helped to strengthen illusions in the lefts, those "friends of the USSR" and to help them to keep control over the trade union movement—a position summed up in the notorious slogan put forward by the Communist Party: "All power to the General Council." It was the General Council of traitors, as was soon to be proved.

Even *after* the betrayal of the general strike, the Bukharin-Stalin leadership clung pathetically to the Anglo-Soviet Trade Union Committee, in spite of repeated snubs. Then, in 1927, when the British government broke off diplomatic relations with the USSR, using "communist propaganda in India" as its pretext, the committee demonstrated its real value as a point of support: the TUC walked out of the committee and denounced the Russians!

The Chinese Revolution

"The Kuomintang, whose principal group entered into an alliance with the Chinese Communists, represents a revolutionary bloc of workers, peasants, intellectuals, and urban democracy on the basis of a community of class interests of these strata in the struggle against the imperialists and the whole militarist feudal order for the independence of the country and for a single revolutionary democratic government."

Resolution of the Comintern Executive, March 1926

THESE WERE also the years of the Chinese revolution of 1925–27, a gigantic upheaval of world-historic importance.

China in the early 1920s was a semi-colonial country dominated by the "spheres of influence" of rival imperialist powers, of which Britain and Japan were at that time the most important. These powers exercised their control through territorial rights that they held in the coastal cities, with their own troops on the ground to enforce these rights, and through ties with the gangster warlords who divided up the country. The most important of these were the "pro-British" Wu Pei-Fu, who controlled much of central China, and the "pro-Japanese" Chang Tso-Lin, who was dominant in the north. There were also many minor warlords, shiftingly attached to one or other of the big sharks. In the south, in Canton, a weak Chinese nationalist government, that of the Kuomintang (KMT) maintained a precarious existence by making alliances with one or other local warlord. In the capital, Peking, the official national government of China was impotent.

The Kuomintang was a bourgeois nationalist party that affected a vague leftist rhetoric. "Its declared aims were Sun Yat-sen's "Three People's Principles": nationalism, democracy (people's rights), and socialism (people's livelihood). No concrete proposals gave content to these vague abstractions. The real aim was military power and it was the offer of Soviet military aid which attracted Sun towards an alliance [with the USSR]."[26] An agreement was reached between the Kuomintang and the government of the USSR in 1923 that led to the dispatch of Russian arms and military and political advisors to Canton the following year. Soon the Kuomintang had a relatively efficient army headed by Chiang Kai-shek, who had received military training in Russia.

The Chinese Communist Party, founded in July 1921, was still tiny in 1923. That January, the Comintern executive resolved that all members of the Chinese Communist Party should enter the Kuomintang as individuals, although at the same time the party "must maintain its independent organization.... While supporting the Kuomintang in all campaigns on the national-revolutionary front, to the extent that it conducts an objectively correct policy, the Chinese Communist Party should not merge with it and should not during these campaigns haul down its own flag."[27] How these mutually incompatible aims were to be achieved was not explained.

On May 30, 1925, the British-controlled and officered Shanghai police fired on a demonstration, killing twelve people. The effect was swift and tumultuous. Shanghai, the great foreign stronghold with its Western banks and mills and its foreign areas, was paralyzed by a general strike. Even servants left foreign homes.... It soon spread.... Incomplete statistics recorded 135 strikes arising directly out of the May 30th shootings, involving nearly 400,000 workers....

At Hankow on June 11, a landing party of British soldiers fired upon a demonstration, killing eight and wounding twelve. In Canton, Chinese seamen employed by British shipping companies walked out on June 18. On June 23, a demonstration of students, workers and military cadets paraded in Canton.... British and French machine-gunners opened fire on the marchers. Fifty-two students and workers were killed and 117 wounded. A boycott of British goods and a general strike were immediately declared. Hong Kong, the fortress of Britain in China, was totally immobilized. Not a wheel turned. Not a bale of cargo moved. Not a ship left anchorage.[28]

This explosion was led by individual rebels and young nationalists—and the Chinese Communist Party. The party grew massively out of it. Soon it had thirty thousand members, compared with fewer than a thousand in 1924, and the overwhelming majority were workers in the coastal cities.

The Chinese working class was very new but already large: about three and a half million workers in the modern, mainly foreign-owned sector of industry, plus another eleven million in small enterprises, mainly Chinese-owned. It was also highly concentrated in a few cities. Before the movement that followed May 30, the unions, new and in many cases led by the communists, counted their members only in thousands. By the end of 1925, they had three million members. At the same time a peasant movement, based on refusals to pay rent, began to grow in adjacent provinces, particularly around Canton.

All this was highly disconcerting for the Kuomintang leaders, now dominated by Chiang Kai-shek since Sun Yat-sen had died in late 1924. They were nationalists. They knew that without mass popular support, they could not hope to break the power of the imperialists and their warlord protégés. So they had to support the protest movements after May 30. But they were bourgeois nationalists, with innumerable family ties among merchants, capitalists, and landowners—groups that in China were closely intertwined. Workers' power and peasant revolt were as frightening to them as to the foreign bosses of Jardine Matheson and the Shanghai and Hong Kong Bank.

So the Kuomintang sought to use, control, and then destroy the mass movement. This was a very difficult operation. It was in fact impossible without two conditions: first, the fast-growing Communist Party must continue to be subordinated to the Kuomintang; second, the Kuomintang needed the continued supply of Russian guns and Russian military expertise that alone could make possible the expansion of a reliable "professional" army for use against workers, peasants, and warlords alike.

The Bukharin-Stalin leadership guaranteed both. When Chiang Kai-shek launched his first military coup in Canton in March 1926 and imprisoned the local Communist Party leaders and strike committee activists (for the strikes were still continuing), the Chinese Communist Party was ordered to submit. In January, the CPSU had declared: "To our party has fallen the proud and historic task of leading the first victorious proletarian revolution of the world.... We are convinced that the Kuomintang will succeed in playing the same role in the East."[29] Now, after the March coup, the subordination of the Chinese Communist Party to the Kuomintang was reinforced.

Thus the Chinese Communist Party was subordinated to the Chinese bourgeoisie in the interests of the foreign policy pursued by the Russian bureaucracy. Stalin's chief emissary in China, Borodin, declared: "The present period is one in which the communists should do coolie service for the Kuomintang."[30] That same month, a right-wing Kuomintang leader, Hu Han-min, was elected to the presidium of the Krestintern and gave fraternal greetings to the sixth plenum of the Comintern executive!

> In March 1926...the sixth plenum of the Comintern executive had sanctified the policy of the "bloc of classes" in China. Chiang's coup had exploded the notion of "community of class interests" on which that policy was based. But the Kremlin leaders, intent upon winning a strong ally in China, overcame this difficulty by ignoring it and concealing the fact that power in Canton had passed into the hands of the extreme right wing of the Kuomintang under the leadership of Chiang Kai-shek. Shortly afterward, the Political Bureau of the CPSU, against one adverse vote—Trotsky's—approved the admission of Chiang's Kuomintang into the Communist International. "In preparing himself for the role of an executioner," wrote Trotsky, Chiang Kai-shek "wanted to have the cover of world communism—and he got it."[31]

Thus strengthened, Chiang ended the boycott of British goods, reestablished ties with British imperialism, and launched the "Northern expedition," an attempt at the military conquest of China. This was greeted with enthusiasm by a wave of peasant revolts, which spread ahead of the Kuomintang army. This army was initially small, only sixty thousand strong—but the numerically superior forces of the warlords disintegrated.

By February 1927, Chiang's troops were nearing the Yangtze River. The Chinese Communist Party launched a general strike in support of the Kuomintang in Shanghai, the largest city still held by warlord troops, and after a bitter struggle the workers seized power there in March. Chiang arrived within days. He proceeded to assemble reliable Kuomintang forces with which to smash the workers' organizations. The Communist Party was under strict orders not to resist—representatives of the Comintern executive had told the Chinese communists to hide their arms and in no case to use them. The party continued to woo Chiang and persuade its supporters that all was well.

On April 12, 1927, the Kuomintang forces struck. This was not simply a repetition of the Canton coup. It was a bloodbath, a massacre. Chiang now wanted to reassure the imperialist powers, whose troops still held the foreign concessions in China, that the Kuomintang was "safe." The Communist Party, the unions, and all traces of workers' organization in Shanghai were completely and thoroughly eliminated.

But even at the thirteenth hour, Bukharin and Stalin would not countenance a break with the Kuomintang. They transferred their allegiance from Chiang to the Kuomintang "left" headed by Wang Ching-wei, which controlled a rival Kuomintang center based on Wuhan. This was now designated the "revolutionary Kuomintang." In less than three months, its leaders had come to terms with Chiang and turned on the communists. Wang Ching-wei was later to become the puppet ruler of Japanese-occupied China from 1938 until his death in 1944.

There was still a large and growing peasant revolt, but the urban workers' movement was now broken. The Communist Party leaders outside the cities, notably Mao Tse-tung and Chu Teh, became leaders of peasant guerrilla bands. The Kuomintang was never, ultimately, able to defeat these peasant bands—but, of course, the class nature of the Chinese Communist Party, which was now based on the peasantry, was transformed. There was one final urban spasm in the struggle. An attempted coup was launched in Canton, where the Communist Party still had a substantial underground organization. It was timed to coincide with the fourteenth congress of the CPSU in December 1927, where the oppositions inside Russia were to be finally proscribed. Its aim was to give Bukharin and Stalin a "victory" to celebrate, and it was led by Stalin's personal emissary, Heinz Neumann. Without political preparation, without genuine support, it was crushed within days. Another massacre of workers followed. The Chinese Communist Party's last working-class support was wiped out.

This then was the final fruit of the period of Bukharin's leadership of the Comintern.

SIX

THE THIRD PERIOD
1928-1934

"No, comrades...the pace must not be slackened. On the contrary, we must quicken it as much as is within our powers and possibilities.... We are fifty or a hundred years behind the advanced countries. We must close this gap in ten years. Either we shall do it, or they will crush us."

Stalin, Speech to Industrial Managers, 1931

BY 1928, the New Economic Policy (NEP) in Russia was entering its final crisis. The oppositions inside the CPSU had been crushed. Trotsky, Zinoviev, and a host of others had been thrown out of the party, and many were in jail or administrative exile. The last remnants of inner-party democracy had been destroyed.

The bureaucracy had allied itself with the forces of petty capitalism in Russia against the oppositions and against the danger of working-class revival—that was the essence of the Bukharin-Stalin bloc.

Now, in the moment of its triumph, it was faced with a *kulak* offensive, the "grain strike" of late 1927. The *kulaks,* the prosperous minority among the peasantry, controlled practically all the marketable grain in Russia, the surplus over and above peasant consumption. They attempted to force prices up by withholding it from sale. "The grain collection in the autumn of 1927, which should have been the best months, yielded less than half the quantities of 1926."[1] In a country that was still overwhelmingly agrarian, this was a catastrophe.

The bureaucracy was driven to resort to forced requisitioning of grain in spring 1928. This undermined the fundamental basis of NEP, provoking massive peasant resistance. It led in turn to the forced collectivization of agriculture and to the adoption by Stalin of the opposition's industrialization program in an extravagantly exaggerated form. The first Five-Year Plan was launched.

And it was launched by Stalin. For the section of the bureaucracy around Bukharin shrank from the massive coercion that was inseparable from the Five-Year Plans. It was, over time, eliminated from power. So too was a section of Stalin's own faction. Stalin became now no longer the spokesman of the bureaucracy, but its master, a despot who "became ever more capricious, irritable and brutal," as his successor, Khrushchev, was to say in 1956.

The USSR was transformed. The last remnants of what Lenin had called in 1920 "a workers' state with bureaucratic deformations" were swept away. The bureaucracy became a self-conscious ruling class. Bureaucratic state capitalism was firmly established—its ideology being, of course, "socialism in one country."

The original Five-Year Plan had assumed that 20 percent of grain-producing peasant households would be collectivized by 1934. In fact, by March 1930, 55 percent overall were collectivized. Then came a temporary halt, signaled by Stalin's "dizzy with success" speech, which blamed "excesses" on local officials. The extent of the coercion involved is indicated by the official (post-Stalin) admission that, in the *three months* following Stalin's speech, the proportion of households collectivized fell to 23 percent. Then came the second offensive, accompanied by mass deportations of both real kulaks and masses of far poorer peasants. By 1934, 71.5 percent of the households and 87.5 percent of the crop area were collectivized.[2]

The result was a decline in the grain harvest from 73.5 million tons in 1928 to 67.5 million tons in 1934, in spite of substantial investment in agriculture. Not until the second half of the 1930s was average grain output back to the levels of the late 1920s. With livestock, which was slaughtered on a huge scale by desperate peasant owners, the situation was far worse. In the official figures (published post-Stalin), the number of cattle was 70.5 million in 1928 and 42.5 million in 1934. Bread rationing was reintroduced in the towns and lasted until 1936.

What is relevant here is not the economic irrationality of the process but the fact that it was only possible through a reign of terror. A vast network of forced labor camps was created, populated in the first instance largely by deported peasants. Their numbers were soon to be supplemented by an influx of workers, technicians, officials, and all manner of people accused of "sabotage," pilfering, and opposition of any kind. By the second half of the 1930s, forced labor—modern slavery—was an important sector of the economy and a most powerful deterrent against any kind of resistance to the new despotism. The sheer scale of this slavery at the height of the Stalinist period—estimates range from a minimum of five million to a maximum of fifteen million—enormously enhanced the rule of the GPU, the political police, and with it the general brutality of the regime.

The working class was transformed. It grew from eleven million, including office staffs, in 1928 to twenty-three million in 1932. As a vast flood of ex-peasants was drawn into the towns and into the rapidly expanding workforce, all residual trade union rights disappeared. The unions became, in fact though not in form, state agencies for disciplining the workforce and speeding up output. This fast-growing workforce was atomized by vicious repression. But not only that. Layers of experienced workers were drawn into management and administration, and a little later, extensive bonus schemes established huge differentials within the workforce itself. *Average* real wages were cut severely. The official (post-Stalin) statistics show a fall of 12 percent between 1928 and 1932, and this is certainly a gross underestimate. But a "labor aristocracy" was created with incomes much larger in relation to the average than in any of the advanced industrial countries. As a political force, the working class no longer existed. The bureaucratic state capitalist totalitarian regime was consolidated.

By these means, Russia was partly industrialized. Steel output, four million tons in 1927–28, had risen to six million tons in 1932. Coal output grew faster, from thirty-five million tons to sixty-four million tons in the same period. Other sectors also showed substantial growth.

The Comintern now existed, for Moscow, as a subsidiary agency for the defense of this process of industrialization and of the bureaucracy that directed it. Any external upheaval, any upset in international relations, anything that might have adverse effects on the foreign trade of the USSR—for the first Five-Year Plan assumed a substantial *increase* in foreign trade—was out. The ferocious "leftism" of the Comintern's Third Period had, paradoxically, the desired effect.

Paradoxically, that is, because a leftist policy might have been expected to throw the communist parties outside Russia into conflict with the governments of their respective countries. The leftism of the Third Period was so extreme, however, that it effectively isolated these communist parties from the working-class movements, making them abstentionist and passive. They, therefore, posed no threat to their ruling classes—and no danger to USSR foreign policy. This was especially true of Germany, where Stalinist foreign policy was based largely on attempts at rapprochement with the Weimar Republic, including its army chiefs, who were given military facilities in Russia that enabled them to evade the restrictions on rearmament imposed by the Treaty of Versailles.

The leftism of this period was not imposed by the Comintern *consciously in order to* isolate the communist parties. The leftist policies, in fact, developed from struggles inside the USSR, where the bureaucracy was now fighting against the right wing around Bukharin. But the result was favorable...the cap fit, so the Comintern wore it.

The new line

"Just as social democracy is evolving through social imperialism to social fascism, joining the vanguard of the contemporary capitalist state...the social-fascist trade union bureaucracy is, during the period of sharpening economic battles, completely going over to the side of the big bourgeoisie...transforming the reformist trade union apparatus into a strike-breaking organization. In this process of the rapid fascistization of the reformist trade union apparatus and of its fusion with the bourgeois state, a particularly harmful role is played by the so-called 'left' wing of the Amsterdam International (Cook, Finmen, etc.) who, under the cloak of opposition to the reactionary leaders of the Amsterdam International, are trying to conceal from the work-

*ers the real significance of the process and are forming an active
and constituent part (and by far not the least important) in the
system of social fascism.* "

Resolution of the tenth plenum of the
Comintern executive, July 1929

THE NEW Comintern line appeared with the Sixth World
Congress in July–August 1928, which proclaimed the end of
capitalist stabilization ("the second period") and the arrival of
"the third period...a period of intense development of the contradictions in the world economy...of the general crisis of capitalism...a fresh era of imperialist wars among the imperialist
states themselves; wars of the imperialist states against the
USSR; wars of national liberation against imperialism; wars of
imperialist intervention and gigantic class battles."[3]

No very clear conclusions were yet drawn from this apoca-
lyptic prospect, perhaps because the supporters of Bukharin
were still fighting a rearguard action—Bukharin's last appearance in the Comintern was at this congress. But this shortcom-
ing was corrected at the tenth plenum of the Comintern
executive in July 1929:

> In this situation of growing imperialist contradiction and
> sharpening of the class struggle, fascism becomes more and
> more the dominant method of bourgeois rule. In countries
> where there are strong social democratic parties, fascism as-
> sumes the particular form of social fascism, which to an ever-
> increasing extent, serves the bourgeoisie as an instrument for
> paralyzing the masses in struggle against the regime of fascist
> dictatorship.[4]

What this farrago of nonsense meant on the ground was the
rejection of the united front—not honestly, of course, but by
way of again proposing united front action "only from below."
The social democrats were now the *main* enemy, not the actual
fascists. The absurdity of the "social-fascist" analysis has already been demonstrated. As to the question of who is the
main enemy, this cannot of course be answered with any time-
less generalizations. It depends entirely on the situation. At the
point where this "new line" really mattered, in Germany at the
time of the rise of Hitler, the main enemy was clearly the fascists of the Nazi Party, not the social democrats of the SPD.

The notion that the trade union bureaucracy was "social fascist" led logically to the notion of splitting the unions, to the establishment of separate "red" unions. But this was not formally argued—because of Lenin's explicit condemnation of "dual unionism." Instead, ultraleft and adventurist policies were pursued that enabled the trade union bureaucracies to drive out the left, which is what happened in Germany, Britain, and the United States, or to isolate the left unions, which is what happened in France and Czechoslovakia. The effect was to strengthen the right in every case.

There was plenty of provocation from the social democrats, plenty of gross class collaboration and heartbreaking sellouts. To take the British case as an example, it is certainly true that after 1926, the TUC leaders acted as "a strike-breaking organization" for many years. So the establishment in 1929–30 of the United Clothing Workers as a breakaway from the National Union of Tailors and Garment Workers, and the United Mineworkers of Scotland as a breakaway from the Miners Federation of Great Britain (now the NUM), was in part a response to the outrageous treachery by right-wing officials. The Communist Party militants who promoted the breakaway unions had an audience, had real if minority support.

But politically it was entirely wrong. The British Communist Party and its Comintern masters not only failed to argue hard, as Lenin had done in 1920, against ultraleftist illusions in "red unions," they encouraged them. The real indictment of the "third period" line of the Comintern on the struggle against the union bureaucracies is that it actually helped the bureaucrats, that it failed to take advantage of such splits between left and right that did occur in the union bureaucracies, that it isolated the militants and their immediate periphery from the mass of trade union members.

The swing to ultraleftism owed something to the need to weaken the impact in the communist parties outside Russia of the opposition criticisms of the previous period's rightist policies, especially after their disastrous outcome in Britain and China. But more important was the need to remove Bukharin's supporters from positions of influence in various communist parties. "The main danger is from the right," it was proclaimed, and the by now well-established techniques of bureaucratically eliminating inconveniently independent party members, pioneered by Zinoviev and developed by Bukharin, were now used ruthlessly against the latter's supporters.

Genuine leftists purged during Bukharin's reign were not, however, reinstated. Instead "leaders of a new type" were promoted and then made the objects of a personality cult mirroring that which now centered on Stalin himself in Russia. Prompt and unquestioning obedience and uncritical worship of Stalin and all his works: these were now the requirements.

Ernst Thälmann of the KPD is a good example of the "new type." "An authentic worker, Thälmann made a good figurehead and enjoyed personal popularity. His other gifts were not outstanding."[5] But he was unfailingly obedient—and that made him leader of the world's largest communist party outside the USSR.

At the Moscow center, Molotov, Stalin's office boy, took over. He had played no part at all in Comintern affairs until 1928.

There was a difference between the "leftism" of the Third Period and that of 1924–25. Then, in spite of the stupidities committed, the Comintern still sought to play a revolutionary role. In 1928–34, this was not so. Extreme verbal radicalism went hand in hand with practical passivity. The communist parties isolated themselves, then shouted furiously from the sidelines.

This suited Stalin well. He still needed these parties, but mainly as propaganda agencies for the USSR. An active policy, for example an approach to the social democrats for an aggressive united front against Hitler, carried the risk of creating political upheavals. This was the last thing Stalin wanted. His policy was conservative: avoid foreign entanglements and so avoid the risk of foreign intervention. The ultraleftism of the Third Period fitted very well with this aim. The Comintern had now ceased to be a revolutionary organization.

Stalin's motives are clear, and in the USSR his word was now law. So why did the Comintern parties accept the new line? Most important was the prestige, inherited by Stalin, of the Russian Revolution—still a fairly recent event. The Soviet Republic was a symbol of hope for communist militants. Defeats in the world outside Russia only strengthened it. The harder the going in other countries, the more important was the myth (as it had now become) of workers' power in Russia, and the prestige of Stalin, "the Lenin of today" as the Stalinist slogan had it. "The darker the night, the brighter the star."

Then, in 1930, came a real and dramatic change in the world situation. When the new line was adopted in the summer of 1928, the world economy was in the full surge of the late 1920s boom, and that boom continued for the first fifteen months of the Third Period. In 1930, following the Wall Street crash of October 1929, a devastating slump developed. Output fell and unemployment rocketed around the world. But in the USSR, the first Five-Year Plan was going forward, output was rising fast, and unemployment, which had been heavy during the NEP period, disappeared. This contrast enormously reinforced the Russian myth and hence Stalin's authority over the Comintern parties.

And in most of these, there was a justifiable revulsion against the excesses of the right turn and its outcome. It was, in general, a revulsion on behalf of a minority, but it gave the Comintern executive, now Stalin's agents, a lever against "rightist" leaderships. Thus the British Communist Party was "turned" with the aid of a leftist opposition centered on the London and Newcastle districts and the Young Communist League.

In most cases though, not much pressure was needed. The big parties—in Germany, France, and Czechoslovakia—had suffered successive purges of rightists, real and alleged, by 1925, then of "leftists," genuine and otherwise, in 1925–27. The survivors in the leaderships had developed supple spines and adapted to the new line and to "leaders of a new type" without too much difficulty. They had successively denounced Trotsky and Zinoviev; now it was Bukharin's turn.

There were exceptions. It proved necessary to expel the rightist majority of the leadership of the American Communist Party by Comintern edict. Those expelled failed to carry the bulk of the membership with them. In Sweden, however, a similar operation against the Kilbom leadership resulted in the secession with Kilbom of the majority of members (about eighteen thousand in 1928). But in most cases, rightist leaders, however prominent, were expelled without taking more than a few of their followers with them.

Membership did fall heavily in many instances. In France, the PCF's claimed membership dropped from 52,526 in 1928 to 39,000 in May 1930, and further to 30,000 in March 1932. The Czechoslovak party, which had claimed 150,000 in 1928, was down to 35,000 in 1931.[6] The British Communist Party had 5,526 registered in March 1928; by late 1929, it claimed 3,500. The Norwegian party, which was a smallish but still significant workers' party in 1928, was reduced to an isolated sect by 1932.

Again, there were exceptions. The South African party had been a small, declining, white-led organization in the late 1920s. With the new line and a new, partly black leadership, it was able to lead a number of strikes of black workers and to gain an influence in spite of repression. Similarly, in Australia, the party was a small propaganda group in the late 1920s. Because the slump hit Australia very hard—one worker in every three was unemployed in 1932—and because the Labor Party was in power and leading the attack on working-class living standards, the ultraleft line fit in with a mood of desperation among sections of the working class. The CPA grew from 249 members in 1928 to 2,824 in 1934, laying the basis for its future influence in the unions.[7]

But the most important case by far was that of the KPD. "From a fairly steady total of 125,000 in the late 1920s, its membership rose to 170,000 in 1930, to 240,000 in 1931, and to 360,000 at the end of 1932 on the eve of catastrophe."[8]

Trotsky, in 1931, called Germany "the key to the international situation." And it was in Germany that the new line was tested in practice by a mass party in a situation of deep and worsening social crisis.

"After Hitler, our turn"

"Herr Brüning has expressed it very clearly; once they [the Nazis] are in power, the united front of the proletariat will emerge and make a clean sweep of everything.... We are not afraid of the fascists. They will shoot their bolt quicker than any other government."

Herman Remmele, KPD Leader,
Speaking in the Reichstag, October 1931

IN THE German federal election of May 1928, the SPD gained 29 percent of the vote, more than nine million votes, a gain of more than 1.3 million over the election of December 1924. The KPD got 10.6 percent of the poll, 3.2 million votes, a gain of half a million, though well short of its May 1924 figure of 12.6 percent of the poll. The Nazis got only 810,000 votes, 2.6 percent of the total. The outcome was a new "great coalition" government of the SPD, the Catholic center party, the liberal democrats, and the right-wing German People's Party, headed by the SPD leader, Hermann Müller.

The new government soon demonstrated its conservative character. It went ahead with the building of the pocket battleship *Deutschland,* although the SPD had vehemently opposed this project during the election campaign. It supported the steel bosses during their lockout in the autumn of 1928. And it pursued a vigorous "law and order" policy, the most notorious example of which was the May Day of 1929.

Karl Zörgiebel, an SPD member and police president of Berlin, forbade demonstrations on May Day. The KPD called one as usual, and it was big, with many SPD members participating. Zörgiebel's police fired on the workers, killing twenty-five and severely wounding another thirty-six. Zörgiebel then defended the police, claiming that the demonstrators had fired first: "Fourteen butts of police rifles had been shattered or pierced by shots from the crowd, though, fortunately, the police suffered no casualties."[9] Zörgiebel was not repudiated by the SPD ministers.

The KPD, therefore, had excellent opportunities to influence and win SPD workers. It proceeded to minimize these opportunities by hysterical ranting about "social fascism," by calling SPD members "little Zörgiebels," and by a total failure to relate to the left-wing opposition in the SPD—which they called the "left social fascists."

Then came the slump.

From 1929 onward, unemployment increased steadily until it reached and passed the six million mark in January 1933. That was the official figure of registered unemployed. Actually, between eight and nine million wage and salary earners were out of work. At the same time, wages and salaries were reduced, unemployment benefit was cut and, owing to the rapid decline of the workers' purchasing power, millions of small shopkeepers, tradesmen, artisans, and peasants were ruined....

> A radical solution, never mind of what sort so long as it was sufficiently radical and effective—that was what an increasing number of Germans wanted in those years until the phrase "*so kann es nicht weitergehen*" (things can't go on like this) was as current as "*guten Tag.*"[10]

In this situation, the KPD needed concrete slogans, effective partial demands with which to influence more and more workers beyond its ranks. Instead, the KPD fed its supporters a diet of talk about "ascending revolutionary struggles," deepening crisis (which everyone could see anyway), the glorious victories of the Five-Year Plan, and the menace of social fascism. It was *politically* passive, notwithstanding its furious propaganda campaigns.

The "great coalition" fell apart at the end of March 1930, the SPD being driven into reluctant opposition because even its right wing could not accept the further cuts in wages and benefits demanded by big business.

Now was the ideal time for the KPD to launch a sustained united front campaign, to put the united front at the center of its political orientation. Against the stupidities of the thesis of "social fascism," Trotsky patiently explained:

> The Social Democracy, which is today the chief representative of the parliamentary bourgeois regime, derives its support from the workers. Fascism is supported by the petty bourgeoisie. The Social Democracy without mass organizations of the workers can have no influence. Fascism cannot entrench itself in power without *annihilating* the workers' organizations....
>
> For the monopolistic bourgeoisie, the parliamentary and fascist regimes represent only different vehicles of domination.... But for both the Social Democracy *and* fascism, the choice of one or the other vehicle...is a question of political life or death....
>
> When a state turns fascist, it doesn't only mean that the forms and methods of government are changed in accordance with the patterns set by Mussolini's...but it means primarily and above all that *the workers' organizations are annihilated:* that the proletariat is reduced to an amorphous state: and that a system of administration is created which penetrates deeply into the masses and which serves *to frustrate the independent crystallization of the proletariat.* Therein precisely is the gist of fascism.[11]

Thus there was an *objective* basis for a united front against fascism, a genuine common interest in preserving independent working-class organizations. Not that Trotsky had any illusions that the SPD and ADGB leaders, left to themselves,

would recognize this. Far from it. But a substantial and growing section of their supporters could and would *if* the KPD
made this central to its politics. And, in order to win SPD-influenced workers, it was necessary not only to address them directly, *but also to address their leaders,* repeatedly and with
concrete proposals at each new turn in the struggle, ignoring
rebuffs, *precisely* to influence the ranks and so to force at least
sections of the SPD/ADGB apparatus into a united front. But
the Stalinized KPD pursued exactly the opposite policy.

After the collapse of the "great coalition," Brüning, the center party leader, took over, ruling by decree as the Weimar con-
stitution allowed, because he lacked a parliamentary majority.

In September 1930, elections were held. For two years,
following the theory of "social fascism," the KPD had concentrated its fire on the SPD. Now it made electoral gains at
the SPD's expense. The KPD got 4,592,100 votes, or 13.1
percent of the total. The SPD's vote was 8,577,700 compared
to 9,153,000 in 1928—a fall from 29.8 percent to 24.5 percent. But at the same time, the Nazis made a spectacular advance, multiplying their 1928 vote by eight times to
6,409,600 or 18.3 percent. Moreover the total vote for workers' parties was down from 40.4 percent to 37.6 percent.
Brüning still lacked a majority but was sustained in office by
the "toleration" of the SPD, which never voted against the
government on a matter of confidence.

The KPD leaders were jubilant. They now had seventy-
seven deputies in the Reichstag instead of fifty-four. They made
light of the Nazis' advance. "September 14th was the high
point of the National Socialist movement in Germany...what
comes after can be only decline and fall," declared the KPD's
daily newspaper in Berlin.[12] As to the danger of fascism coming
to power: "The fascist dictatorship is no longer a threat, it is
already here,"[13] it said, meaning that the Brüning regime was
fascist, just as its social democratic–led predecessor had been.

It was a combination of blindness, ultraleft bombast, and
parliamentary cretinism.

Trotsky's sober and accurate criticism was written that
same September of 1930:

> From the viewpoint of "normal" parliamentary mechanics,
> the gain of 1,300,000 votes is considerable, even if we take

into consideration the rise in the number of voters. But the gain of the party pales completely beside the leap of fascism from 800,000 to 6,400,000. Of no less significance for evaluating the elections is the fact that the social democracy, in spite of substantial losses, retained its basic cadres and still received a considerably greater number of workers' votes than the KPD.

Meanwhile, if we should ask ourselves what combination of international and domestic circumstances could be capable of turning the working class toward communism with greater velocity, we could not find an example of more favorable circumstances for such a turn than the situation in present-day Germany.... If the KPD, in spite of the exceptionally favorable circumstances, has proved powerless to seriously shake the structure of social democracy with the aid of the formula of "social fascism," then real fascism now threatens this structure....

No matter how true it is that the social democracy prepared this blossoming of fascism by its whole policy, it is no less true that fascism comes forward as a deadly threat to that social democracy.... There can be no doubt that, at the crucial moment, the leaders of social democracy will prefer the triumph of fascism to the revolutionary dictatorship of the proletariat. But precisely the approach of such a choice creates exceptional difficulties for the social democratic leaders among their own workers. The policy of the united front of the workers against fascism flows from this whole situation. It opens up tremendous possibilities for the KPD. A condition for success, however, is the rejection of the theory and practice of "social fascism," the harm of which becomes a positive menace under the present circumstances.[14]

This, however, was precisely what the KPD leaders could not do. Stalin had decreed the theory of social fascism, and only he could scrap it. There were indeed certain shifts in emphasis in the line. In January 1931, the slogan of a "people's revolution" was advanced as the "chief strategic slogan of the party"—an attempt to outbid the Nazis in nationalist demagoguery. The slogan "strike at social fascism, then you will hit national fascism" was declared "too simple" in May, and so on and so forth. But the central thrust of the line was maintained—the SPD is the main enemy.

Thus when the Nazis promoted a referendum to dismiss the social democratic provincial government in Prussia in the summer of 1931, the KPD supported the move, called it the "red referendum" and did its best (unsuccessfully as it turned out) to destroy the government in circumstances in which the *only* alternative government was a Nazi-conservative coalition.

In 1932, the KPD found itself in a bloc with the Nazis in support of an unofficial transport workers' strike in Berlin.

> Street collections were organized for strike funds, and in some districts of Berlin, the unique spectacle could be observed of a Communist and a Nazi standing arm in arm and shouting in an agreed rhythm, while they were shaking their collection boxes: "For the strike fund of the NSBO (Nazi union fraction), For the strike fund of the RGO (Red trade union opposition)." The sight of this perverted united front was so repulsive to most ordinary trade unionists that the initial sympathy for the strikers turned into disgust and hostility.[15]

As a result, the strike quickly collapsed and the isolation of the KPD from the mass of social democratic workers was massively reinforced.

Thälmann, as late as September 1932, four months before Hitler became chancellor of Germany, repeated obediently:

> The Trotskyists put forward the slogan of unity of the SPD with the KPD to divert the desire for unity among the masses into fake political channels...precisely at the present stage in Germany the two [the SPD and the Nazis] appear in their true colors as "twin brothers," as Comrade Stalin acutely emphasized...our party has of late been combating with great success all tendencies to weaken the struggle in principle against social democracy and has fought with all severity against all conceptions that the main offensive within the working class ought no longer to be directed against social democracy.[16]

In fact, the KPD's policies *strengthened* the position of the SPD leadership among SPD-influenced workers. But the line was pursued to the bitter end. As has been noted, the KPD continued to grow, but its social weight did not increase. The proportion of factory workers among its membership, as reported by the Comintern's organizational director in 1932, declined as follows: 1928, 62.3 percent of the membership; 1929, 51.6 percent; 1930, 32.2 percent; 1931, 20.22 percent.[17] Part of this was the inevitable result of the slump, but much of it was not. The party was increasingly a party of the unemployed and the declassed. Its vote continued to grow also. In the last free elections (November 1932), it got 5,980,000 votes (16.9 percent) to the SPD's 7,248,000 (20.4 percent), and the Nazis'

11,737,000 (33.1 percent).

But votes were not decisive. The KPD's practical passivity, the rubbish of "social fascism," the blindness to reality; these were decisive. In 1930, 1931, even 1932, a vigorous united front policy could have defeated Hitler. Stalin's Comintern ensured that such a policy was not pursued.

Why? It was certainly not in the interests of the Stalinist bureaucracy in the USSR that the Nazis should come to power, smash the KPD as well as the SPD and the unions, undertake a massive rearmament program, and then set out, consciously and deliberately, to break the power of Britain and France in Europe and to dominate and exploit the continent. This would *inevitably* involve an attack on the USSR itself—which it did in 1941. Moreover, this program was set out openly in Hitler's book *Mein Kampf*, written as early as 1923. So how could Stalin be so blind?

There are two reasons. The first is simple ignorance. Stalin, immensely shrewd and ruthless as a machine politician, understood little of the realities of the class struggle outside Russia. His notorious aphorism of 1924, twice referred to already, is worth quoting in full here: "Fascism is the fighting organization of the bourgeoisie buttressed on the active support of social democracy. Social democracy is effectively the moderate wing of fascism."[18] Hence "they are not antipodes but twins."

Of course there were those, even at the center of the Comintern apparatus, who recognized this for the garbage that it was. Thus Palmiro Togliatti, a former disciple of Gramsci and later to be leader of the Italian Communist Party in the period after the Second World War, had given an excellent analysis of the relationship and fundamental conflict of interest between social democracy and fascism as late as the Sixth World Congress of the Comintern in 1928, when the ultraleft line was already ascendant.

Togliatti was a man of great ability but, like Gramsci, he could not conceive of a policy independent of the Russian leadership. Hence he "made haste to prove that, precious as truth was to him, Molotov was more precious, and...he wrote a report in defense of the theory of social fascism. 'The Italian Social Democracy,' he announced in February 1930, 'turns fascist with the greatest readiness.' Alas, the functionaries of official communism turned flunkies even more readily," wrote Trotsky.[19] Indeed, purged and purged again by 1929, most of them had turned flunky long before.

The second and more important reason was the desperate anxiety of all sections of the bureaucracy, including those less than enthusiastic about Stalin's rule, concerning their isolation from *any* other section of Russian society. They could not fail to recognize, in principle, that the mass of the population—workers as well as peasants—were violently hostile to the immense privations imposed upon them by the first Five-Year Plan. The regime was far, far more isolated than it had been in 1919. Foreign intervention now might be fatal, since it might draw this so far largely passive hostility together. So *any* upheaval abroad was unwelcome—and the Russian bureaucracy still saw Britain and France, who had sent troops to Russia during the civil war after the revolution, as the main enemies.

Thus *Pravda* rejoiced after the elections in Germany in 1930 that the Nazi successes created "not a few difficulties for French imperialism."[20] The desperate hope that an extreme right-wing government in Germany would be principally anti-French dominated their thinking.

So passivity was forced on the KPD. A challenge to Thälmann's authority as early as the summer of 1928 by the majority of the KPD central committee, no less, was overruled by the Comintern executive. (This was the Wittart affair: various close associates of Thälmann had been involved in theft of party funds and he had covered up for them.) Later, in 1931–32, Neumann and Remmele, who had been elevated to the top leadership of the KPD by Moscow, were eliminated in their turn. They had, within the framework of the "new line," fought for too active a policy by the KPD. And an active policy of any kind was anathema to Moscow. Thälmann, Stalin's mouthpiece, had to be upheld.

So Hitler came to power without resistance in January 1933. True, his first cabinet contained only a minority of Nazis; his party had only about one-third of the votes at the previous election in November 1932. But all this was irrelevant. Once in power and confident that the workers, deeply divided between the SPD and the KPD, would not actively unite against him, he proceeded to outlaw first the KPD, then the

SPD, then the unions. There was no effective resistance to the reign of terror unleashed by his Nazi storm troopers. After eliminating the workers' parties, he got the rump of the Reichstag to elect him dictator. What followed was not "our turn," but our destruction: the workers' movement was smashed and the class atomized. Trotsky summed up the experience a few days after Hitler became chancellor:

> The history of the German working class represents the most tragic page of modern history. What shocking betrayals by its historical party, the Social Democracy! What ineptitude and impotence on the part of its revolutionary wing! But there is no need to go so far back. For the past two or three years of the fascist upsurge, the policy of the Stalinist bureaucracy has been nothing else but a chain of crimes which literally saved reformism, and thereby prepared for the subsequent successes of fascism.[21]

SEVEN

THE TERROR AND
THE PEOPLE'S FRONT

*"In 1937, new facts came to light regarding the fiendish crimes
of the Bukharin-Trotsky gang.... The trials showed that these
dregs of humanity, in conjunction with the enemies of the people, Trotsky, Zinoviev and Kamenev, had been in conspiracy
against Lenin, the Party and the Soviet state ever since the early
days of the October Revolution.... The trials brought to light the
fact that the Trotsky-Bukharin fiends, in obedience to the wishes
of their masters—the espionage services of foreign states—had
set out to destroy the party and the Soviet state, to undermine
the defensive power of the country, to assist foreign military interventions, to prepare the way for the defeat of the Red Army,
to bring about the dismemberment of the USSR...and to restore
capitalist slavery in the USSR."*
History of the Communist Party of the Soviet Union, 1938

IN JANUARY 1934, the seventeenth congress of the Communist Party of the Soviet Union was held. According to the
official history, "The seventeenth party congress is known
in history as the 'Congress of Victors.'" It celebrated "the victory of socialism in all branches of the national economy
[which] had abolished the exploitation of man by man."[1] Such
fantasies aside, the Stalinist bureaucracy did have something to
celebrate. The *kulaks* had been "liquidated as a class," the
mass of the peasantry was now firmly penned into the collective farms and, above all, industrial output had risen massively—the official claim was a 70 percent increase, on
average, since 1928. The bureaucracy was now firmly en-
trenched in power and privilege.

But behind the unanimity—there was no debate; all resolutions were carried unanimously—and the paeans of praise for the "great leader and teacher," Stalin, there were tensions. The mass of workers and collectivized farmers were inert, numbed, but labor productivity was very low by the standards of the West. Sections of the bureaucracy began to doubt whether this extremely dangerous state of affairs could be remedied simply by continued police terror. Some favored a greater reliance on incentives and a certain relaxation of coercion. Rightly or wrongly, views of this sort were attributed to S. M. Kirov, member of the Politburo and boss of the Leningrad region.

On December 1, 1934, Kirov was murdered. His death was the signal for unleashing a new wave of state terrorism that was to last for five years. Unlike its predecessor of 1929 onward, this terror was not *primarily* directed at workers and peasants, although they inevitably made up a large proportion of its victims. It was directed by Stalin at the bureaucracy itself, with the object of reducing all ranks of the hierarchy to total, unquestioning obedience to his will.

Stalin held no government position in 1934. His authority, so far as it rested on any "legal" basis, derived entirely from his position as general secretary of the Russian Communist Party. In theory, however, this post was subject to election. Any session of the—now large—central committee could depose him. More immediately, the ruling Politburo, which was theoretically a subcommittee of the central committee, could suspend him and recommend his replacement. It was therefore vital for Stalin that he establish an unassailable ascendancy over his immediate associates in the Politburo. Hence the vast "conspiracies" unearthed by his successive police chiefs, Yagoda, Yezhov, and Beria. (The first two were themselves executed as traitors during Stalin's reign, the third was shot immediately on Stalin's death on the orders of his successors.)

At a deeper level the great purges, and the show trials that were their spectacular accompaniment, marked the decisive repudiation of the October Revolution through the physical destruction of those who had been involved in it. All the "old Bolsheviks" were eliminated. Significantly the soviets, long dead in practice, were in 1936 replaced by conventional electoral districts. A new ruling class was consolidating itself—and that involved the destruction of all those who had even the most tenuous connection with the revolutionary past.

The fate of the "victors" of 1917 was revealed by one of those who survived, Stalin's successor Khrushchev, in 1956: "Of the 139 members and candidates of the party's central committee who were elected at the seventeenth congress, 98 persons, i.e., 70 percent, were arrested and shot.... Of 1,966 delegates with either voting or advisory rights, 1,108 persons were arrested on charges of anti-revolutionary crimes."[2]

Aside from a handful of token survivors of the revolutionary years, these people were Stalinists: in addition to Kirov, probably murdered on Stalin's orders, at least six other members of Stalin's handpicked Politburo were shot before 1940. But politically, the imaginary crimes of which these men were convicted were attributed to the influence and orders of the former leaders of *opposition* to Stalin, above all to the archfiend Trotsky. In the three great show trials of August 1936, January 1937, and March 1938, surviving leaders of the revolution, including Zinoviev, Kamenev, and Bukharin, were induced to confess that on Trotsky's orders they had organized conspiracies to "restore capitalism" in the USSR.

For Stalin to consolidate his power internationally, it was essential that the Comintern parties be immunized against criticism from the revolutionary left. For the Comintern was now to be swung, by Stalin's agents, to a position well to the *right* of the social democratic parties, to a position of class collaboration—precisely the position taken by the social democrats during and after the First World War and against which the founders of the Comintern had revolted. The "People's Front," systematic class collaboration with the "liberal" bourgeoisie, was now the order of the day—again, in the interests of Stalin's foreign policy. The international campaign against "Trotskyism," which came to include not only the genuine article but also any left-wing tendency, which looked, however hesitantly, toward the traditions of the first five years of the Comintern, was intensified, especially from 1935, precisely because in these years the now degenerated Comintern sought to pull the working-class movement far to the right. Those who resisted were denounced as "Trotsky-fascists," and Trotsky himself was branded as Hitler's agent.

The show trials, the anti-Trotsky campaigns, and the new line of the "People's Front" were inseparably connected. The numerous social democrats, liberal intellectuals, and assorted "progressives" who supported the People's Front also—with few exceptions—defended the Moscow Trials and the anti-Trotsky hysteria. That was logical enough. Not only did fear of Hitler drive them toward Stalin, but they were joining with Stalin in trampling down a revolutionary tradition, that of Marx and Lenin, that they hated and feared. It is no accident that in this period the Stalinized communist parties were able to attract, for the first time, masses of middle-class members and sympathizers.

On this basis, some of the Comintern parties were able to register considerable growth and new parties were built. Thus in Latin America, where the Chilean Communist Party had been the only substantial party in the 1920s, and had then been decimated by repression, the Comintern was able to claim in 1935 affiliated parties in Colombia, Costa Rica, Peru, Puerto Rico, and Venezuela, as well as substantial growth in the previously tiny parties in Argentina, Brazil, Cuba, and Mexico. All these parties grew on the basis of the new policy of class collaboration.

The People's Front in France

"Today the situation is not what it was in 1914. Now it is not only the working class, the peasantry, and all working people who are resolved to maintain peace, but also the oppressed countries and the weak nations whose independence is threatened by war. The Soviet Union, the invincible fortress of the world proletariat and the oppressed of all countries, is the focal point of all the forces fighting for peace. In the present phase, a number of capitalist states are also concerned to maintain peace. Hence the possibility of creating a broad front of the working class, of all working people, and of entire nations against the danger of imperialist war."
Resolution of the Comintern Executive, April 1936

HITLER IN power soon denounced the Treaty of Versailles, which restricted the German army to a maximum of one hundred thousand men, and launched a massive rearmament drive.

Manifestly he was preparing for war, and the USSR was obviously one of his intended victims. Stalin now sought military alliances with the then still-dominant powers of Europe: Britain and France.

The "People's Front" line was wholly and solely designed to bring pressure to bear on these governments and any others that might be induced to join a military coalition with the USSR against Hitler. The seventh and last world congress of the Comintern in July–August 1935 was summoned to promote this end: "The struggle for peace opens up before the communist parties the greatest opportunities for creating the broadest united front," it declared.

> All those interested in the preservation of peace should be drawn into this united front. The concentration of forces against the chief instigators of war at any given moment (at the present time—against fascist Germany and against Poland and Japan, which are in league with it) constitutes a most important tactical task...the establishment of a unity front with social democratic and reformist organizations...with mass national liberation, religious-democratic, and pacifist organizations and their adherents, is of decisive importance for the struggle against war and its fascist instigators in all countries.[3]

Of course this was not the united front tactic. It was not a question of class politics at all but of mobilizing support for the foreign policy pursued by Stalin, support from any class and, in particular, from the ruling classes of other countries. The Comintern had come full circle. From breaking with the social democrats because of their nationalist, class-collaborationist policies, the Comintern was now more openly concerned with class collaboration than most social democrats.

It was no longer even a question of subordinating the working class of a semi-colonial country to a supposedly "progressive national bourgeoisie" in the alleged interests of the struggle against imperialism—which had been itself a policy directly contrary to the decisions of the Comintern's second congress. It was now a matter of subordinating the working classes *and* the national movements to the rulers of the two greatest colonial empires on earth, Britain and France!

A most significant feature of the seventh congress of the Comintern was the careful avoidance of anti-imperialist speeches, which had still featured prominently at the sixth. No delegate from India spoke, the first time this had happened since 1919, nor from Indonesia. The speech of a delegate from Egypt (then British-controlled), who had obviously been called in error, was omitted from the official record. Delegates from the French colonies of Syria and Vietnam did speak, but managed to avoid all reference to French imperialism! With the adoption of the "People's Front" line, the Comintern got a new manager. George Dimitrov, the Bulgarian exile who had worked in Germany throughout the Third Period and gained prestige by his defense at the trial of those accused of the Reichstag Fire, now took over. He was a vigorous and effective advocate of the new turn, not a mere hack.

In May 1935, the USSR signed a "mutual security pact" with France. The PCF, which had only recently been shouting the ferocious rhetoric of the Third Period and calling the French government fascist, now swung right around. Maurice Thorez, its leader, proclaimed: "The peace policy of the Soviet government is in conformity with the historic instructions of Lenin; it is firmly conducted by Stalin; it corresponds to the interests of the international proletariat...there is, for the moment, a correspondence of interest between bourgeois France and the Soviet Union against Hitler."[4] But Stalin (rightly) distrusted the French conservative government, which was then headed by Pierre Laval, a future collaborator with Hitler. The PCF pressed for a "People's Front" to contest the next elections, which came in the spring of 1936. Its call fell on fertile soil.

A revulsion against Third Period cretinism had arisen independently of Moscow. The effect of Hitler's victory inside Germany was to create a groundswell for working-class unity among politically conscious workers. Those communist parties that still had some serious working-class support inevitably felt this groundswell. Some Communist Party leaders were, even before their line changed, casting around for ways to reduce the isolation of their parties without actually falling foul of the Comintern center. And the socialist parties too were becoming open to the appeal for unity.

In France, the shift began in 1934. On February 6, the fascist organizations staged a riot and attack on the Chamber of Deputies (parliament) in an attempt to force the government to resign. After the fighting with the police, there were thirteen dead and more than three hundred seriously injured. The reformist CGT called for a mass strike and demonstration on the 12th. The CGTU called for a mass strike and demonstration on the 12th. The CGTU, after a sharp conflict at the top, endorsed the call. The strike was well supported in Paris, and the two organizations' separate demonstrations finally merged.

Pressure for a united front grew. Hesitantly, the PCF leadership began to shift. Thorez was in Moscow in May and seems to have gotten permission for some sort of approach to the SFIO for united action against the fascists. The SFIO leaders were also under pressure from their own ranks. That same February 1934 the Austrian clerical reactionaries used the army to smash the Socialist Party and the unions and established a military police dictatorship. The SFIO leaders were seriously alarmed and so, after various maneuverings, a pact was signed at Ivry between the two parties for united action against the fascists.

In October, negotiations began for fusion between the CGT and the CGTU. The CGTU had lost its majority position, in terms of workers organized, through its Third Period antics. Final agreement to fuse was not reached until 1936, but the fact that unity was in the air helped both federations to grow.

Such developments were so far confined to workers' organizations. Soon, however, the Radicals, the main bourgeois center party, were drawn in, together with some smaller groupings. The Popular Front was born as an electoral alliance, on a vaguely "progressive" but definitely nonsocialist platform that stressed "collective security," in other words, military strength. It won the elections of April/May 1936 easily. On the second ballot, the SFIO got 182 deputies, the Radicals 116, and the PCF, campaigning on the slogan "for a strong, free and happy France," got 72.

"We boldly deprived our enemies of the things they had stolen from us and trampled underfoot. We took back the Tricolor and the Marseillaise," said Thorez.

Both the workers' parties increased their vote over that in 1932; the SFIO from 1,950,000 to 2,206,000; the PCF from 800,000 to 1,468,000. The Radicals, as well as the right, lost ground. Leon Blum, the SFIO leader, formed the Popular Front government with the enthusiastic support of the PCF. But the PCF had no ministers. Thorez had wanted to bargain for representation, but, in their different ways, both Stalin and Blum thought it inadvisable to alarm the bourgeoisie with supposedly "red" ministers. The PCF accepted without dispute. Shortly after the election, events took a turn none of the leaders expected. The slump had come late to France, but it had struck hard, and was used by the employers as an opportunity to cut wages. Now, with the electoral defeat of the right and a certain economic revival, there was a great explosion of strikes and sit-ins. More than six million workers were involved in June. Total union membership, a little over a million in the spring (CGT, eight hundred thousand; CGTU, three hundred thousand) shot up to over five million in the summer. The strike wave was not simply economic. All manner of demands for job control, for nationalization, for fundamental change were put forward. It was a real "festival of the oppressed." Unorganized workers with no previous experience of struggle—including insurance workers and bank clerks—occupied their workplaces. In some cases, the occupations started before any actual demands had been formulated!

Trotsky, from his exile in Norway, wrote: "The French Revolution has begun." The left-wing SFIO leader, Marceau Pivert, proclaimed: "Everything is possible." Now was the time for a revolutionary socialist party to generalize the workers' struggles into a fight for workers' power. But the PCF was no longer a revolutionary party.

The bourgeoisie, terrified, appealed to Blum. Blum appealed to Thorez. Everyone understood that to control the upsurge by mere promises was impossible. Real concessions had to be made. So the bosses, most of whom a few weeks earlier would not have even considered recognizing a union, now hurried to agree with the union chiefs a "new deal," including union recognition, sweeping wage rises, and the forty-hour week—a sensational gain at the time. But would these large-scale concessions be sufficient to damp down the workers' militancy? So wide and deep was the ferment that the SFIO and CGT leaders could not control it alone. In selling this "Matignon Agreement" to the workers, the PCF played the decisive role.

The PCF, which only a year earlier had been talking of "ascending revolutionary struggles" whenever there was a local strike, and calling (most inappropriately) for "soviets everywhere," was regarded by the newly awakened workers as the real "red" party. Its membership shot up to more than one hundred thousand.

But its new authority was used not to develop, but to *end* the movement. "It is necessary to know when to end a strike," declared Thorez. "Everything is *not* possible," declared the party's daily paper. It was "Trotskyism" to persist, and "Trotskyism," as had been proved in Moscow, was an agency of the fascists. Some of the strikes and occupations spluttered on for a while, but the PCF was able to kill the movement.

It is worth stressing the distance between the policies adopted by the PCF in its Popular Front period and the tactic of the *united* front as it had been understood in the early years of the Comintern. Whereas the second congress had spelled out the importance of communists maintaining their political independence, the PCF suspended all criticism of its socialist allies. Whereas "unity" had been understood as practical agreements for particular *action* designed to test the reformist leaders in the eyes of their supporters, it now came to mean an electoral bloc that tested no one. And whereas cooperation between revolutionaries and others had once centered around *workers* and their organizations, on the basis that revolutionaries had to achieve a majority in the working class, the PCF now extended its passive, uncritical unity to the organizations of the bourgeoisie. In the name of antifascism, the interests of workers were subordinated to those of the French ruling class.

The Popular Front did not only squander an opportunity to establish workers' power; as the bourgeoisie began to recover its confidence, the government shifted rightward. So did the PCF. By the end of the year, it was calling for the transformation of the "People's Front" into a French Front, by the inclusion of those right-wing conservatives who were strongly anti-German on nationalist grounds.

Blum started, cautiously at first, to erode the gains made by workers in the Matignon Agreement. Demoralization began to set in the working class.

Blum was then replaced as premier by the Radical Party leader, Camille Chautemps. The PCF supported Chautemps, who in turn supported the bosses—much more openly than had Blum. And when Chautemps was himself replaced by the more conservative Édouard Daladier, the PCF continued in its support. This was finally withdrawn in September 1938, not because of any change in internal policy but because, in that month at Munich, the British and French governments agreed to sacrifice their ally Czechoslovakia to Hitler in the hope of buying him off. "Collective security," the supposed foreign policy of the Popular Front and the very reason for its existence in the eyes of Stalin and the PCF, was unceremoniously junked. The USSR was isolated. Then, and only then, did the PCF deputies vote against the government, still nominally the Popular Front government, in a vote of confidence.

By this time, the working-class movement was in full retreat. Demoralization was widespread. Union membership was falling substantially. Hitler was going from strength to strength. The smell of defeat was everywhere. In late September 1939, that same Chamber of Deputies, with its Popular Front majority, outlawed the PCF! Then, in June 1940, the same bloc voted to install the quasi-fascist regime of Philippe Pétain and Laval. Thus ended the Popular Front in France.

On one issue, and one only, had the PCF been critical of the Popular Front governments from the outset: on the issue of selling arms to the Spanish Republic. Because the French and British ruling classes supported Franco, Blum and the rest always refused to sell arms to be used against him. The PCF, and Stalin, wanted the Spanish Republic to survive—but as a bourgeois republic under a Popular Front government. In Spain as in France, the Popular Front policy led to a crushing defeat for the working class.

The Spanish Revolution

"The Spanish proletariat displayed first-rate military qualities. In its specific gravity in the country's economic life, in its political and cultural level, the Spanish proletariat stood, on the first day of the revolution, not below but above the Russian proletariat at the beginning of 1917. On the road to its victory, its own organizations stood as the chief obstacles.... The 'republican' military commanders were more concerned with crushing the social revolution than with scoring military victories. The soldiers lost confidence in their commanders, the masses in the

*government; the peasants stepped aside; the workers became
exhausted; defeat followed defeat; demoralization grew
apace.... By setting itself the task of rescuing the capitalist
regime, the Popular Front doomed itself to military defeat....
Stalin succeeded completely in fulfilling the role of grave digger
of the revolution."*

Trotsky, *The Lessons of Spain: The Last Warning*, 1937

THE SPANISH People's Front included four bourgeois parties—the Republican Union, the Republican Left, the Catalan
Nationalists, and the Basque Nationalists—plus the Spanish
Socialist Party (PSE), the Communist Party (PCE), and the
POUM, a party that claimed to be revolutionary but was in
fact centrist. It owed its electoral victory in February 1936 to
the tacit support of the anarchists, who controlled Spain's
biggest trade union federation, the CNT. The new government
was headed by Manuel Azaña, a moderate conservative, former war minister and former prime minister, whom the PCE
had been denouncing as a fascist until 1935. It was at first
composed entirely of ministers from the bourgeois parties.

"Perhaps the most remarkable feature of the [Popular
Front] program was the absence of any serious social and economic demands," noted a shrewd bourgeois historian, E. H.
Carr. "Agitation for the taking over of the land by peasants
and of the factories by workers was actively pursued by the
left.... But this was not reflected or encouraged in the program
of the popular front. In terms of the heated controversies of the
day, it was a mild and anodyne document, evidently designed
to rally a wide coalition of divergent interests and sectors of
opinion, united only in their commitment to the republic and
to some form of democratic government."[6]

However, various things do have to be taken into account:
the Spanish monarchy had been overthrown only in 1931, and
the conservative right was by no means reconciled to its passing; one concrete measure that the Azaña government
promised and actually fulfilled on their accession to power was
an amnesty for political prisoners, some thirty thousand of
them, overwhelmingly left-wingers and the majority anarchists;
and "democracy" meant very different things to the Spanish
bourgeoisie—most of whom were strongly opposed to the

amnesty—and to the class-conscious sections of the working class and the peasantry.

The Popular Front government was very moderate, but nevertheless its accession sparked off a wave of strikes, land seizures by peasants, and popular violence against hated representatives of the far right. Azaña had taken over from an ultra-right-wing government whose repression had radicalized both workers and peasants. The size of the strike wave gives some idea of the upsurge: a million workers were on strike on June 10, falling to half a million ten days later, but rising to a million again early in July.

Law and order were breaking down. The situation was becoming revolutionary in spite of efforts to calm things down by ministers, the Socialist Party, and still more the Communist Party.

On July 17, a military coup was launched, supported by the fascists, the hierarchy of the Catholic Church, and practically the whole of the upper classes, which had lost confidence in the ability of Azaña to control the situation. Azaña himself, who had been president since May, knew of the coup in advance, as did at least some of his ministers. They kept quiet about it.

When the army garrisons and civil guard units tried to take over the major cities, there was the most spectacular spontaneous working-class rising ever seen. Starting in Barcelona on July 19, it led to the defeat of the garrisons over a large part of Spain. The top leaders of the workers' parties played little part in it: the action was led mainly by local anarchist and socialist militants. Now the party leaderships moved to reassert control—and the Spanish Communist Party was on the extreme *right* wing of this movement.

"It is absolutely false," declared Jesus Hernandez, editor of the Communist Party's daily paper, "that the present workers' movement has for its object the establishment of a proletarian dictatorship after the war has terminated. It cannot be said that we have a social motive for our participation in the war. We communists are the first to repudiate this suggestion. We are moved exclusively by a desire to defend the democratic republic."[7]

That republic had ceased to exist. The government had practically no military or police forces at its disposal. The soldiers were either with General Franco and the fascists or had gone over to the workers' militias, which were now the only armed force outside the still-limited territory held by Franco. The government lacked even an effective administrative apparatus; workers' committees had taken over there too.

> As soon as you cross the frontier, you are halted by armed men. Who are these men? Workers. They are militiamen—that is, workers with their normal clothes—but armed with rifles or revolvers and with signs on their arms indicating their functions or the power they represent.... They are the ones who...will decide...not to let you in or to refer it to the "committee."
> The committee is the group of men who are in charge over in the next village and who exercise complete power there. It is the committee who see to the normal municipal functions, who formed the local militia, armed it, and supplied it with food and lodging from the funds raised by a levy imposed on all the local inhabitants. They are the ones who give you permission to enter or leave the town, who closed down the local fascist shops and who carried out essential requisitions.[8]

In short, the situation was similar to that in Russia in March 1917 or Germany in November 1918.

Those who described themselves as "we communists" now set out to *re-create* the bourgeois republic, just as the SPD leaders had done in Germany in 1918. They did so with the aid of the Socialist Party and its bourgeois allies. Not that the latter represented much. The Communist Party made a coalition "with the shadow of a bourgeoisie," as Trotsky said, for the real bourgeoisie was now with Franco.

Franco's military threat was serious, of course, but the People's Front actually helped him recover from the setback of the workers' rising. In July and August 1936, Franco relied heavily on Moorish troops flown in from Spanish Morocco in German transport planes. His mobile field army was built, initially, around this Moorish core. Now there had been a massive rebellion in Morocco (in both French and Spanish colonies) in the 1920s led by Abd-el-Krim. This rebellion had taken years to suppress. An immediate declaration of Moorish independence by the Spanish republican government would have undermined what was temporarily Franco's main resource and caused his Moorish troops to waver, at the very least. Abd-el-Krim himself, a prisoner of "comrade" Blum's French People's

Front, appealed to the Spanish Socialist Party leader Largo Caballero to intercede with Blum to secure his release—so that he could return to Morocco to fight against Franco.

It was out of the question. Independence for Spanish Morocco would inevitably bring renewed rebellion in French Morocco. But the whole purpose of the People's Front was to cement a deal between the French and British Empires and the USSR. So the Moorish troops, offered nothing, stayed with Franco.

The Moroccan question was not exceptional. On all other issues, even those of a directly military nature, winning the war was sacrificed to the vain hope of closer relations with the governments of Britain and France. So the navy, most of which had mutinied at the beginning of the war and gone over to the republic, was kept in harbor by the republican government for fear that its deployment might offend the rulers of France and Britain—for these countries had joined with Germany and Italy in mounting naval patrols to enforce "non-intervention" in Spain, a non-intervention directed entirely against the republic.

As with the PCF in France, the Spanish Communist Party fought for the counterrevolution in its bourgeois-democratic form, in the name of "democracy" and "the struggle against Trotskyism and fascism." As the Spanish party was initially very weak—it had about one thousand members in 1934, rising to thirty-five thousand in February 1936, and 117,000 in July 1937—it depended heavily on Russian and Comintern support. The USSR maintained a carefully regulated supply of arms and ammunition to the republic and was virtually the only supplier, since the British government and the Popular Front government in France came to an agreement with the fascist powers, Germany and Italy, to prevent arms supplies. The Comintern's contribution was the International Brigades; about forty thousand men in all, of whom ten thousand were French.[9] Again, this very significant military contribution was a powerful aid to the influence of the Spanish Communist Party. The heroism of the volunteers, Communist Party members and others, was tragically exploited in the interests of Russian foreign policy.

But the Spanish Communist Party did not depend solely on this. It also built itself a middle-class base:

The small manufacturers, artisans, tradesmen, peasant proprietors, and tenant farmers, in their immense majority, placed their hopes of a better life, not in the abolition, but in the accumulation of private property. To develop as they wished, they needed freedom of trade, freedom from the competition of the large concerns now collectivized by the labor unions, freedom to produce goods for personal profit, freedom to cultivate as much land as they pleased, and to employ hired labor without restriction. And above all, they needed, in order to defend that freedom, a regime in their own image, based on their own police corps, their own courts of law, and their own army; a regime in which their own power would be unchallenged and undiluted by revolutionary committees. But now all hope of such a regime had gone, and the middle classes had no alternative but to withdraw into the background. They were far too prudent to swim against the tide, and even adapted their attire to suit the changed conditions. "The appearance of Madrid," observed a right-wing Republican, "was incredible: the bourgeoisie giving the clenched-fist salute.... Men in overalls and rope sandals, imitating the uniform adopted by the [working-class] militia; women bare-headed...."

But floundering in the flood of the revolution, the liberal as well as the conservative members of the middle classes were impressed at the time only by the manifest impotence of their parties and soon began to cast about for an organization that would serve as a breakwater to check the revolutionary tide set in motion by the Anarchist and Socialist labor unions.

They did not have to search for long. Before many weeks had passed the organization that succeeded in focusing upon itself their immediate hopes was the Communist Party....

The Communist Party was soon to mold decisively the course of events in the camp of the anti-Franco forces. Championing the interests of the urban and rural middle classes—a stand few Republicans dared to assume in that atmosphere of revolutionary emotionalism—the Communist Party became within a few months the refuge, according to its own figures, of 76,700 peasant proprietors and tenant farmers and of 15,485 members of the urban middle classes. That its influence among these layers went far beyond these aforementioned figures is indubitable, for thousands of members of the intermediate classes in both town and country, without actually becoming adherents of the party, placed themselves under its wing. From the very outset of the revolution, the Communist Party, like the PSUC, the Communist-controlled United Socialist Party of Catalonia, took up the cause of the middle classes who were being dragged into the vortex of the collectivization movement or who were being crippled by the disruption of trade, the lack of financial resources, and by the requisitions carried out by the working-class militia.

"In a capitalist society, the small tradesmen and manufacturers," declared *Mundo Obrero*, the Communist organ in Madrid, "constitute a class that has many things in common with the proletariat. It is of course on the side of the democratic Republic, and it is as much opposed to the big capitalists and captains of powerful fascist enterprises as the workers. This being so it is everybody's duty to respect the property of these small tradesmen and manufacturers.

"We therefore strongly urge the members of our party and the militia in general to demand, and, if need be, to enforce respect for these middle-class citizens, all of whom are workers, and who therefore should not be molested. Their modest interests should not be injured by requisitions and demands that are beyond their meager resources."

".... It would be unpardonable," said *Treball*, the Communist organ in Catalonia, "to forget the multitude of small commodity producers and businessmen of our region. Many of them, thinking only of creating what they had believed would be a position of independence for themselves, had succeeded in setting up their own businesses. Then came a change in the situation precipitated by the attempted coup d'etat of the fascists. The immense majority of small commodity producers and businessmen, who had lived completely on the margin of events, are now more confused than anyone, because they feel that they are being harmed and that they are at an obvious disadvantage in comparison with the wage earners. They declare that nobody is concerned about their fate. They are elements who might tend to favor any reactionary movement, because in their opinion anything would be better than the economic system that is being instituted in our region....

"The distressing situation of many of these people is obvious. They cannot run their workshops and businesses because they have no reserve capital; they have hardly enough to eat, especially the small manufacturers, because the wages they have to pay to the few workers they employ prevent them from attending to their own daily needs....

"A moratorium must be granted to all those people who have placed themselves at the service of the antifascist militia, so that they do not have to bear the full weight of the requisitions imposed by the war. A moratorium must be granted and a credit should be opened so that their businesses do not go into liquidation."

As a means of protecting the interests of the urban middle classes in this region, the Communists organized eighteen thousand tradesmen, handicraftsmen, and small manufacturers into the Federación Catalana de Gremios y Entidades de Pequeños Comerciantes e Industriales (known as the GEPCI), some of whose members were, in the phrase of *Solidaridad Obrera*, the CNT organ, "intransigent employers, ferociously anti-labor," including Gurria, the former president of the Tailoring Trades Association.

Because the Communist Party gave the urban and rural middle classes a powerful access of life and vigor, it is not surprising that a large part of the copious flow of new members into the party in the months following the revolution came from these classes. It is almost superfluous to say of course that these new recruits were attracted, not by Communist principles, but by the hope of saving something from the ruins of the old social system. Furthermore, in addition to defending their property rights, the Communist Party defined the social overturn, not as a proletarian, but as a bourgeois democratic revolution. Within a few days of the outbreak of the war, Dolores Ibárruri, the woman Communist leader, known as La Pasionaria, declared in the name of the Central Committee:

"The revolution that is taking place in our country is the bourgeois democratic revolution which was achieved over a century ago in other countries, such as France, and we Communists are the front-line fighters in this struggle against the obscurantist forces of the past."[10]

It took two years of complicated maneuvers to end the dual power of 1936 and restore control over the working class to the bourgeois republic,[11] two years in which Franco was able to conquer much of Spain using conventional warfare. Without the political line of the People's Front to destroy the revolution, Franco's prospects would not have been good. But the workers' revolution was strangled by the People's Front before Franco defeated the republic, with a victory in March 1939 that established a right-wing dictatorship that was to last nearly thirty years.

The Spanish Communist Party had used its influence both to support the bourgeois ministers against the socialists and to support the right-wing socialists against the left-wing majority of the Spanish Socialist Party (PSE), the anarcho-syndicalists, and the POUM.

First the POUM was denounced as Trotskyist (which it was not) and then, in 1937, it was suppressed, along with the left wing of the anarcho-syndicalists. Many were murdered; the GPU operated freely under Spanish Popular Front protection.

The left-wing socialists, including the prime minister, Caballero, were driven out of the government. Regular police forces were reestablished and bourgeois property rights reasserted. In the army, the officer corps reclaimed its supremacy. The militias were absorbed or disbanded. The conquests of 1936 were progressively taken back. In the end, the reconstituted bourgeois state machine, in the person of General Segismundo Casado, overthrew the government and surrendered to Franco in March 1939. Stalinism had destroyed the Spanish Revolution.

The last spasm, 1939–43

"The definite passing over of the Comintern to the side of the bourgeois order, its cynically counterrevolutionary role throughout the world, particularly in Spain, France, the United States, and other 'democratic' countries, created exceptional supplementary difficulties for the world proletariat."

Trotsky, *The Transitional Program*, 1938

IN AUGUST 1939, Stalin reversed his foreign policy. Despairing of an effective military alliance with Britain and France, he made a pact with Hitler on August 23. Its basis was the partition of Poland between Germany and the USSR, the absorption of the Baltic states of Estonia, Latvia, and Lithuania by the USSR, and a pledge of Russian neutrality in the coming war. The war started one week later. The German Army invaded Poland on September 1. By September 3, Germany was at war with Britain and France. But Stalin stood by his pact with the Nazis. On September 17, the Russian Army crossed the border into Poland to seize Stalin's share of the booty.

The Comintern center did not immediately react to the new situation. Presumably it had not been told what to say. At any rate, the British and French communist parties did not immediately change course. Although greeting the Hitler-Stalin Pact as "a triumph of the great Socialist Republic's peace policy,"[12] they supported their own governments on the outbreak of war. The French Communist Party deputies voted for the war with more enthusiasm than those of most other parties—while the British Communist Party leader Harry Pollitt rushed out a pamphlet entitled *How to Win the War*.

But it soon appeared that this was not at all what was wanted. Moscow decreed that the "antifascist alliance" was now out. Another somersault was imposed on the Comintern parties. Early in November 1939, the Comintern executive declared:

> The ruling circles of England, France, and Germany are waging war for world supremacy. This war is the continuation of many years of imperialist strife in the camp of capitalism. Three of the richest states—England, France, and the U.S.— hold sway over the most important routes and markets. They have seized possession of the main sources of raw materials. In their hands are huge economic resources. They hold over one half of mankind in subjection. They cover up the exploitation of the working people, the exploitation of the oppressed peoples, with the false phantom of democracy, so all the more easily to deceive the masses.
>
> Fighting against their world supremacy, and for their own mastery, are the other capitalist states, which came later into the arena of colonial expansion. They want to divide anew, to their own advantage, the sources of raw materials, food, gold reserves, and the huge masses of people in the colonies. Such is the real meaning of this war, which is an unjust, reactionary, and imperialist war.... *The working class cannot support such a war* [against Germany].[13]

The Comintern had, of course, been saying the opposite of this since 1935!

The sheer cynicism and effrontery of this abrupt reversal of position shook the British and French communist parties particularly. Twenty-one PCF deputies had already resigned from the party after the announcement of the Hitler-Stalin Pact. Members and fellow travelers now deserted both parties in droves, even before the outlawing of the PCF. In Britain, Pollitt had to resign his position as party leader and look for work in his trade.

But the core of the parties held firm. The myth of the "socialist fatherland," the suspicion that the motives of the rulers of Britain and France were indeed exactly as the Comintern statement described them (which was, indeed, well-founded), the belief that Stalin was somehow outwitting Hitler, the complete Stalinization of the party machines and the long-established habits of obedience all served to ensure that the new turn was accepted.

It should not be thought that it represented a return to the revolutionary position of the Comintern's early years. Far from it. The cry now was for peace, in other words for a negotiated peace with Hitler and the Nazis on the basis of the new status quo—which of course included the possession by the USSR of half of Poland and of the Baltic states. It coincided with the "peace efforts" of Hitler's foreign office in two periods especially: immediately after the conquest of Poland and again in the summer of 1940 after the defeat of France, when Hitler launched his own "peace offensives."

Less than two years later, events forced on Stalin yet another reversal of foreign policy. Hitler's forces invaded the USSR. The Comintern again obediently fell into line (without a word of explanation for the change), calling for "the mobilization of every force of the nations embattled against Hitler in a life and death struggle."[14] The war that on June 21, 1941, was an imperialist war in Britain and France became a war for democracy on the 22nd.

The Comintern now ceased to have any significance for Stalin. The thing had served its purpose. Churchill and Roosevelt, representing the ruling classes of the West, now Stalin's allies, did not like anything that might remind *their* workers of the revolutionary years—even if only in name. In May 1943, the executive committee of the Comintern called for its dissolution. In June, it announced that this had been "unanimously agreed" upon by the sections. On June 8, 1943, the Comintern was formally liquidated.

Stalin commented, in an interview with the Moscow correspondent of the Reuters news agency, as follows:

> *Question:* British comment on the decision to dissolve the Comintern has been very favorable. What is the Soviet view on this matter?
>
> *Answer:* The dissolution of the Comintern is proper and timely because it facilitates the organization of the common onslaught of all freedom-loving nations against the common enemy—Hitlerism…. It facilitates the work of patriots of all countries for uniting the progressive forces of their respective countries, regardless of party or religious faith, into a single camp of national liberation.[15]

"Patriots," "freedom-loving nations"—and Marx had written that all history is the history of *class* struggles! The Comintern's formal liquidation had come long after its death as a revolutionary workers' international.

The liquidation of its leading personnel had also come earlier. The Bolshevik Party, the driving force of the Comintern in its early years, had a central committee of twenty-four members in 1917. Of these, seven died before Stalin established his dictatorship and two, Stalin himself and Alexandra Kollontai, were still alive in 1943. *All* the other fifteen were murdered, with or without "trial," by the Stalinist regime. They included all the Bolshevik representatives on the Comintern executive in the early years: Bukharin, Radek, Trotsky, and Zinoviev—the only exception is Lenin.

The entire leadership of the Polish Communist Party, which had taken refuge in the USSR or had in some cases been summoned there, perished in the great purge of the 1930s. Warski, Walecki, and Wera Kostrywa, from the party's right wing, Domski and Unslicht of the left, and even the Stalinist Lenski, who had been general secretary since 1929—all were liquidated. The only prominent members of the party who survived were those, among whom Gomulka was notable, who had the good fortune to be serving long sentences in Polish prisons at the time. The Polish party itself was dissolved by Stalin's agents in 1938.

The German communists fared little better. Wilhelm Pieck, a founding member of the KPD, was preserved as a figurehead. Otherwise, those prominent KPD leaders who had taken refuge in the USSR were murdered. They included Hugo Eberlein, the only German delegate at the Comintern's 1919 congress and a long-serving member of the Comintern executive. Of the three who led the KPD in the notorious Third Period, Neumann and Remmele were murdered in the USSR; Thälmann died in a Nazi concentration camp.

Most of the leaders of the Eastern European parties who were in the USSR were also arrested and shot or sent to die in concentration camps by Stalin. Tito, later to be ruler of Yugoslavia, testified long afterward: "In 1938 when I was in Moscow...we were discussing whether to dissolve the Yugoslav Communist Party or not. All the Yugoslav leaders at that time in the Soviet Union had been arrested. I was alone."[16]

Similarly, most of the Hungarians, including Béla Kun, the Finns, including Kullervo Manner, head of the short-lived Finnish Socialist Republic of 1918 and then a member of the Comintern executive, the Latvians, including J. A. Berzin, who had been at Zimmerwald and signed the declaration of the Zimmerwald Left, also disappeared. Of the major illegal parties, only the Italians, most of whose leaders were in exile in France after Mussolini's takeover, and the Chinese, who now controlled a territory of their own in part of China, escaped. For all the others, taking refuge in the "socialist fatherland" from repressive regimes in their own countries meant death.

Stalin sought to destroy the revolutionary Marxist tradition both physically and politically, as the leading representative of the new ruling class in Russia.

EIGHT

THE LEGACY OF THE COMINTERN

THE COMINTERN had been founded in 1919 as a consistently *internationalist* organization, heir of the Zimmerwald Left, hostile to *every* ruling class and to the "disintegrating admixtures of opportunism and social-patriotism" inside the working-class movement.

When it was dissolved in 1943 it was, and had been for the best part of a decade, an instrument of *nationalist* policies that aimed to mobilize working-class support for various ruling classes against other ruling classes. It had carried "opportunism and social patriotism" to new depths.

In 1919, the Comintern had stood for uncompromising working-class struggle. In 1943, it stood, and had stood for years, for systematic class collaboration with various bourgeois and petty-bourgeois forces, *subordinating* working-class interests to theirs according to the shifting requirements of Russian diplomacy.

At its foundation, the Comintern had declared its opposition to *all* imperialisms and proclaimed the right of self-determination of all peoples. By 1943, indeed earlier, it had come to oppose the national struggle in the colonies and "spheres of influence" of Russia's allies. Thus, when the Indian National Congress launched its "Independence Now" campaigns in British-ruled India in 1942, the Communist Party of India denounced the congress leaders as "traitors" and "Japanese agents." The congress leaders, who included Gandhi and Nehru, were imprisoned by the British. The CPI leaders did their utmost to damp down the mass agitation that followed, which included mass strikes and riots, and defended every act of repression by the British authorities. In 1943, Stalin, Roosevelt, and Churchill came to an agreement at Tehran to repartition the world between them into the new spheres of influence. The USSR had itself joined the ranks of the imperialist powers.

In 1919, the Comintern stood unequivocally for workers' revolution and workers' power based on a system of workers' councils: "The victory of the working class lies in shattering the organization of the enemy power and organizing workers' power; it consists in the destruction of the bourgeois state machine and the construction of the workers' state machine," declared the 1919 *Platform*. All this was explicitly abandoned with the 1935 congress and was never revived. Trotsky called it "the Comintern's Liquidation Congress." The Comintern parties heaped unblushing praise on Stalin's brutal, despotic dictatorship *over* the working class in the USSR. The Comintern had become simply an instrument of the class rule of the Russian bureaucracy.

The wheel had come full circle. The Comintern had come to reject all that it had set out to fight for. This was not a matter of merely tactical changes to adjust to changing circumstances—although, of course, this argument was constantly used to justify each new betrayal. Internationalism, workers' power, anti-imperialism; these are not tactics, but principles, necessary conditions for the successful struggle for socialism. It was because the social democratic parties had abandoned them that the Comintern was founded in the first place.

Inevitably, given the outcome, many people question the validity of the tradition represented by the early Comintern: does it contain some original taint, flaw, or distortion that led to, or at any rate facilitated, its becoming a tool of Stalin's foreign policy?

The old myth of the "original sin" of Bolshevism, going back to 1902, of the monolithic party controlled from the top by a single will, does not stand critical examination—which does not, of course, prevent it being presented as an indisputable truth by a wide range of socialism's opponents. In fact, as even a cursory acquaintance with its history will show, the Bolshevik organization was anything but monolithic. It experienced sharp internal conflicts that were resolved by argument, sometimes in public, and by voting at congresses. More than once Lenin, the supposed "dictator," found himself in a minority. Moreover his own views on party organization changed and changed again as the circumstances within which the party worked changed.[1]

More serious is the argument that the Comintern imposed unsuitable forms of organization, inspired by Russian conditions, on the parties outside Russia—and that this was a major cause of their ultimate degeneration. As we have seen, Lenin himself was uneasy in 1922 about a tendency to copy mechanically from the Russian experience.

Most critics, however, locate the alleged deformation earlier than 1922. For them, the root of the evil are the twenty-one conditions of 1920. Thus, Claudin, a former leader of the Spanish Communist Party, describes the twenty-one conditions as

> a model of sectarianism and bureaucratic method in the history of the working-class movement...[they] signified in practice that the Communists were organizing a split in the labor movement, and were doing this, moreover, in a mechanical way and not through a political and ideological process that would have enabled the working people to convince themselves that it was necessary.... A large number of socialists and trade unionists who wanted to join the Comintern because they were in sympathy with the Russian Revolution and shared, generally speaking, the revolutionary objectives of the new International, nevertheless disagreed with it on certain points, especially where structure and methods of work were concerned.[2]

Consider these objections seriously. "Organizing a split in the labor movement?" But the main split in the labor movement occurred in August 1914, nearly five years before the Comintern was founded, when the largest social democratic parties repudiated the internationalist position they had voted for at the Stuttgart and Basel congresses of the Second International and backed "their own" governments in the slaughter of the First World War. Were Liebknecht, Luxemburg, Connolly, Maclean, Lenin, Trotsky, Debs, and the rest "sectarian" in refusing to support the war? Was Liebknecht sectarian when he declared "the main enemy is at home"? Was Connolly sectarian when he declared "neither King nor Kaiser?" Was Lenin sectarian when he wrote in 1914: "The worst possible service is being rendered to the proletariat by those who vacillate between opportunism and revolutionary Social Democracy...by those who are trying to hush up the collapse of the Second International or to disguise it with diplomatic phrases."[3]

The International collapsed in 1914. The split followed that collapse. The responsibility for both lay wholly with the social democratic right. The split was further deepened by the out-and-out counterrevolutionary actions of the SPD leaders in Germany in 1918.

That was the decisive split, the central division from which others followed.

What Claudin and his like object to is the subsequent split with the centrists in 1920. In a political sense, this had already occurred at Kienthal in 1916, but in 1920 some of the centrist parties had had "an influx of revolutionary workers." *These* had to be won, and to win them a split with the vacillating, half-hearted, and often treacherous centrist leaders was essential. Hence the twenty-one conditions. Specifically, there *had* to be a break with Ramsey Macdonald, Karl Kautsky, Leon Blum, and other leaders who were willing to use the rhetoric of revolutionary socialism but were far from it in action. Otherwise the movement ran the risk of a repeat of August 1914.

But perhaps the twenty-one conditions had undesirable side effects? It is not necessary for us to idealize them. Cobbled together rather hastily—there were nineteen on the eve of the second congress, two being added at the last moment—they were a fairly blunt instrument, *but they were effective in their main object*. Not all the centrist leaders were excluded, as we have seen, but the worst scoundrels were. The "disagreements on certain points" that Claudin speaks of were in fact disagreements about fundamentals. As to "a political and ideological process," what else were the debates at Halle and Tours? The Comintern at this time had no "bureaucratic" means whatsoever available to it in Central and Western Europe, unlike the centrists and the social democrats. And, in truth, the twenty-one conditions were never fully implemented by *any* communist party in the revolutionary period, often for bad reasons, sometimes for good ones. Claudin's argument is spurious.

Of course, the real issue here is "Moscow domination," not the conditions themselves. The difficulty is real enough. The decline of the Russian Revolution and then the Stalinist counterrevolution that followed did indeed destroy the Comintern. That is indisputable. But, as has been argued repeatedly, the

fates of the revolution and of the International were inseparable, and *necessarily so*. Any scheme for a revolutionary International *separate* from Soviet Russia—and it still was *Soviet
Russia* in 1920—was an utterly utopian proposition.

Moreover, it must be reiterated that in the early years the
Comintern executive's advice was decidedly superior to that of
the various "anti-Moscow," "autonomist" factions in the various parties. Look at the record. Was "Moscow" wrong in its
assessment of the French, German, and Norwegian centrist
leaders? Was it wrong to fight hard against the sectarians, both
those of the passive propagandist variety such as Pannekoek
and Wynkoop or those of the adventurist type such as Béla
Kun, Fischer, and Thalheimer? Of course not.

Was it wrong, in 1921, to argue that the revolutionary
wave had passed, that a retreat was necessary, that the united
front tactic should now be central? Of course not.

Naturally it is possible to point to blunders. The split with
the Italian centrists could doubtless have been better handled.
The perspective of the Red International of Labor Unions was
mistaken and, by 1921, this should have been recognized and
the necessary conclusions drawn. But on the main issues, on
the central thrust of its political line, the Comintern leadership
was right and *all* its opponents, in their different ways, were
wrong. That is precisely why the heritage of the first four congresses, in principles, in strategy, and in tactics, is so indispensable to revolutionary socialists today.

It would be wrong, of course, to apply the letter of Comintern decisions in a mechanical fashion regardless of circumstances. But the essential principles are there. If, for example, a
detailed examination of the balance of class forces, the state of
workers' organizations, the strength of the reformist parties,
show that united front work is relevant, then basic guidelines
for such work can be learned from the early years of the Comintern. It is as necessary today as it was then that any united
front should center around agreements for unity in *action* of
some kind rather than for propaganda; that a prior condition
should be the existence of an independent and politically clear
revolutionary party; and that the push for unity must not
imply the covering up of differences on essentials. These things
we know, not just from the revolutionary experience of the

years following the First World War, of which the first four congresses of the Comintern were the summation, but also from the disasters that followed the *people's fronts* of the 1930s—when these principles were *not* applied.

1923 was the turning point. It saw the defeat of the German October, the beginning of the Russian bureaucracy's growth to self-consciousness, the emergence of the Left Opposition, and the violent bureaucratic reaction to it.

Up to the end of 1923, the Comintern, in spite of inevitable weaknesses and errors, was a genuine workers' International. Its focus was still working-class struggle. The mistakes that were made were, as we have seen, the result of political immaturity and a misreading of the balance of class forces rather than any shifting of that focus. But with the rise of the bureaucracy and the formulation of the doctrine of "socialism in one country," the class focus began to change. In China, in 1925, the Comintern looked to the Kuomintang, an organization of the bourgeoisie, for revolutionary change, not to the workers' organizations alone.

In the period 1924–28, the Comintern became a "centrist" body—Trotsky coined the term "bureaucratic centrism" to describe its policies—though it still carried, with increasing distortions and degeneration, something of the tradition of its revolutionary years. After 1928, the last remnants of these were progressively liquidated, just as the last remnants of workers' power in the USSR were liquidated.

Neither outcome was inevitable. Had the German working class been able to take power in 1923, the future of Europe, the USSR, and the world would have been very different. That "tide which taken at the flood leads on to fortune" was missed, so a new class rule took over in the USSR, inflicting the evils of Stalinism on the working-class movement and reinforcing social democracy in reaction to these.

What remains relevant is the critique of Comintern policy in Britain, China, Germany, and elsewhere put forward by the Left Opposition. That critique, continued by Trotsky after his exile from the USSR in 1929, informs the approach of this book. It is a continuation of the authentic communist tradition.

In 1929, Trotsky wrote: "The thread of history often breaks, then a new knot must be tied. And that is what we were doing at Zimmerwald."[4] That is what he also sought to do with the International Left Opposition and, after 1938, the Fourth International. But although the tradition *was* continued in a living form, it was by an organization whose working-class base was minuscule and in a period when there was little successful mass working-class struggle from which to learn and on which to build.

Those who carried this tradition were to be subjected to a trial that Trotsky had not anticipated. After 1944, Stalinism massively expanded—on the basis of military conquest and agreements with the ruling classes of the West. There were, in fact, three separate and related developments. First, most of Eastern Europe was conquered by the armies of the USSR and incorporated in its "sphere of influence" in the postwar carve-up of Central Europe. Then, in 1947–48, these were transformed *from the top down* into more or less close replicas of Stalin's Russia. Second, the communist parties in the West pursued, until the outbreak of the Cold War in 1947, policies of class collaboration that were, if it were possible, to the right even of the People's Front period. They grew massively and were represented in the governments of France, Italy, Belgium, Denmark, and a number of other countries, including Batista's Cuba. Third, in Albania and Yugoslavia in 1944, in China in 1948–49, and later in Vietnam and Cuba, regimes essentially similar to that of the USSR were established by military means, by the conquest of weak native bourgeois regimes—which had been essentially puppets of foreign powers—by peasant armies led by intellectuals.[5]

These three processes were not clearly distinguished by the groups that made up the Fourth International. A contributory factor to this disorientation was Trotsky's refusal to accept that a counterrevolution had taken place in the USSR and his insistence that the USSR was still some form of workers' state, however distorted. This meant that during the Cold War, when Stalinism was putting forward a view of the world divided into two opposing camps, socialism versus imperialism, the Fourth International groups were drawn into a similar worldview—of workers' states versus imperialism. This led most of them into a position of "critical support" for Stalinism and, since it now seemed that a "workers' state" could be created by means other than working-class revolution, to the adoption in varying degrees of political ideas that looked to some agency other than the working class for the achievement of socialism. Thus they came, in practice, to jettison much of the core of the communist tradition, the tradition of the revolutionary Comintern that Trotsky himself had fought and died to uphold.

For that tradition is concerned with socialism as the *self-emancipation* of the working class. Its essentials are uncompromising internationalism, unconditional support for workers' struggles against *every* ruling class, the goal of a workers' state based on workers' councils as the agency of the transition to socialism, and unequivocal rejection of all suggestions that any other class, alliance of classes, political grouping, or party can substitute for the working class in bringing socialism.

Out of the fight to apply and develop that tradition *in the course of working-class struggles,* a new workers' International will be born. It will necessarily "stand on the ground of the first four congresses" of the Comintern. The circumstances of the 1980s are much more favorable for the rebirth of the international revolutionary workers' movement than they have been for many years.

The Stalinist movement internationally is in an advanced state of disintegration. The Stalinist states themselves are wracked with internal class conflict—the *Solidarnosc* events of 1980–81 in Poland being only the most spectacular example. Their relationships with one another are often tense to the point of barely concealed or open conflict, which at times has resulted in armed clashes—between Russia and China in the 1960s or China and Vietnam in 1982—or even invasion and conquest, as with Vietnam and Cambodia. The myth of a "socialist camp" is tattered indeed and the ideological consequences of this are profound. The communist parties elsewhere, including the important Japanese Communist Party, are in decline and are, in any case, increasingly difficult to distinguish from their social democratic rivals.

The social democratic organizations, caught up in the renewed crisis of capitalism, face increasing difficulties. Social democratic governments of the 1980s in France, Spain, Portugal, and Greece demonstrate merely their impotence to solve the economic crisis or even to alleviate it.

That crisis, which also affects the Stalinist states in varying degrees, must over time intensify the class struggle, whatever temporary depressing effects it might have. The productive potential of the world economy is vastly greater than it has ever been. The world working class is bigger than ever before. The difficulties facing us are immense, of course. But they are capable of solution. Workers' revolution and workers' power are not utopias. They are the only way forward for humanity.

NOTES

Introduction to the 1985 Edition

1. V. I. Lenin, *Collected Works*, vol. 26 (Moscow: Progress Publishers, 1963-70), 465.
2. Lenin, *Collected Works*, vol. 28, 24.
3. Lenin, *Collected Works*, vol. 29, 58.
4. Leon Trotsky, *Writings 1932–33* (New York: Pathfinder Press, 1970), 51–52.

Chapter 1: The Beginnings

1. Quoted in Jane Degras, *The Communist International 1919–43: Documents*, vol. 1 (London: Oxford University Press, vol. 1, 1956; vol. 2, 1960; vol. 3, 1965), 16.
2. Ibid., 6.
3. Lenin, *Collected Works*, vol. 28, 455.
4. Sebastian Haffner, *Failure of a Revolution: Germany 1918–19* (London: Andre Deutsch, 1973), 152. Chris Harman, *The Lost Revolution* (London: Bookmarks, 1982) gives by far the best account of these days and of events in Germany till 1924.
5. Lenin, *Collected Works*, vol. 21, 40.
6. Julius Braunthal, *History of the International*, vol. 1 (London: Thomas Nelson and Sons, 1966), 196–97.
7. Carl E. Schorske, *German Social Democracy 1905–17* (New York: John Wiley and Sons, 1965), 3.
8. Daniel Bell, *Marxian Socialism in the United States* (Princeton, NJ: Princeton University Press, 1967), 71–72.
9. Wolfgang Abendroth, *A Short History of the European Working Class* (London: Monthly Review Press, 1972), 56–57.
10. Quoted in John Riddell, ed., *Lenin's Struggle for a Revolutionary International* (New York: Monad Press, 1984), 76–77.
11. Leon Trotsky, *My Life* (New York: Pathfinder Press, 1970), 233.
12. Quoted in Riddell, *Lenin's Struggle*, 103. Emphases in the

original.

13. Quoted in Sidney Hook, *Toward the Understanding of Karl Marx* (London: London School of Economics, 1933), 32.
14. Quoted in J. H. Plumb, *England in the Eighteenth Century* (London: Pelican Books, 1963), 97.
15. Abendroth, *Short History*, 57.
16. Lenin, *Collected Works*, vol. 21, 242–43.
17. Trotsky, *My Life*, 249.
18. Lenin, *Collected Works*, vol. 21, 387.
19. Lenin, *Collected Works*, vol. 22, 178–79.
20. Franz Borkenau, *World Communism* (Ann Arbor: University of Michigan Press, 1962), 91–92.
21. A. Ramos Oliveira, *A People's History of Germany* (London: Victor Gollancz, 1942), 93.
22. Ibid., 97.
23. Degras, *Communist International*, vol. 1, 19.
24. Quoted in Lenin, *Collected Works*, vol. 25, 393.
25. Lenin, *Collected Works*, vol. 29, 11.
26. Degras, *Communist International*, vol. 1, 13.
27. Trotsky, "What Is Centrism?" in *Writings 1930* (New York: Pathfinder Press, 1975), 237.

Chapter 2: The Mass Parties

1. Lenin, *Collected Works*, vol. 31, 206.
2. Degras, *Communist International*, vol. 1, 109.
3. Ibid., 172.
4. Lenin, *Collected Works*, vol. 31, 21.
5. Degras, *Communist International*, vol. 1, 170.
6. *Workers of the World and Oppressed Peoples Unite: Proceedings and Documents of the Second Congress, 1920* (New York: Pathfinder Press, 1991), 186. *The Second Congress of the Communist International*, vol. 1 (London: New Park Publications, 1977), 247, gives this version: "But splits are not something to undertake lightly. I can imagine a situation where a split is necessary. The proof of that is the USPD in Germany. But that is a bitter necessity. Before splitting one should try to win the workers for a fundamentally clear attitude. For that one needs time and patience. It is much easier to split the workers than it is to win them and hold them together for the revolution in Germany."
7. *Proceedings of Second World Congress*, 184.
8. Ibid., 217–18.
9. Lenin, *Collected Works*, vol. 31, 250–51.
10. Trotsky, *The First Five Years of the Communist International*, vol. 1 (London: New Park Publications, 1974), 97.

11. Quoted in *Proceedings of Second World Congress*, 65.
12. Ibid., 66–67.
13. Trotsky, *First Five Years*, 98.
14. Quoted in *Proceedings of Second World Congress*, 56–57.
15. Quoted in Braunthal, *History of International*, vol. 2, 175.
16. Quoted in *Proceedings of Second World Congress*, 55–56.
17. Quoted in Degras, *Communist International*, vol. 1, 129, 131.
18. Quoted in Solidarity Aberdeen, *Spartakism to National Bolshevism: The KPD 1918–24* (Aberdeen, Scotland: Solidarity UK, 1970), 9.
19. Quoted in Lenin, *Collected Works*, vol. 31, 40.
20. Ruth Fischer, *Stalin and German Communism* (London: Geoffrey Cumberlege, 1948), 108.
21. Quoted in Lenin, *Collected Works*, vol. 31, 40.
22. Quoted in Degras, *Communist International*, vol. 1, 146–47.
23. Ibid., 152.
24. Ibid., 153–54.
25. Fischer, *Stalin and German Communism*, 119.
26. Quoted in Degras, *Communist International*, vol. 1, 82.
27. Fischer, *Stalin and German Communism*, 134. Von Seeckt was the Chief of Staff of the new German Army.
28. See Tony Cliff, *Lenin*, vols. 1 and 2 (London: Pluto Press, 1975 and 1976) and also Grigory Zinoviev, *History of the Bolshevik Party* (London: New Park Publications, 1973).
29. Lenin, *Collected Works*, vol. 31, 258.
30. Ibid., 263.
31. Tom Bell, *The British Communist Party* (London: Lawrence and Wishart, 1937), 67–68.
32. Lenin, *Collected Works*, vol. 31, 72.
33. Quoted in John M. Cammett, *Antonio Gramsci and the Origins of Italian Communism* (Stanford, CA: Stanford University Press, 1967), 132.
34. Institute of Marxism-Leninism, Central Committee of the C.P.S.U., *Outline History of the Communist International* (Moscow: Progress Publishers, 1971), 61.
35. Lenin, *Collected Works*, vol. 31, 149–50.
36. Quoted in Degras, *Communist International*, vol. 1, 160.
37. Lenin, *Collected Works*, vol. 31, 140–41.
38. Marx and Engels, *Selected Correspondence* (London: Lawrence and Wishart, 1934), 351.
39. Lenin, *Collected Works*, vol. 22, 278.
40. Quoted in Degras, *Communist International*, vol. 1, 141.
41. Lenin, *Collected Works*, vol. 31, 241–42.
42. Degras, *Communist International*, vol. 1, 143–44.
43. E. H. Carr, *The Bolshevik Revolution*, vol. 3 (London: Pelican Books, 1966), 263.

44. Degras, *Communist International*, vol. 1, 170.
45. A. Adler, ed., *Theses, Resolutions and Manifestos of the First Four Congresses of the Third International* (London: Ink Links, 1980), 214–15.
46. Adler, *Theses, Resolutions and Manifestos*, 216.

Chapter 3: The Ebb

1. Degras, *Communist International*, vol. 1, 230.
2. Lenin, *Collected Works*, vol. 33, 63.
3. Quoted in Degras, *Communist International*, vol. 1, 243.
4. Ibid., 249–50.
5. Lenin, *Collected Works*, vol. 33, 208.
6. Gwyn Williams, *Proletarian Order* (London: Pluto Press, 1975), 68.
7. Quoted in Degras, *Communist International*, vol. 1, 188.
8. Paolo Spriano, *The Occupation of the Factories* (London: Pluto Press, 1975), 65.
9. Trotsky, *First Five Years*, vol. 1, 262.
10. Quoted in Degras, *Communist International*, vol. 1, 190.
11. Ibid., 193.
12. Cammett, *Antonio Gramsci and Origins*, 121.
13. Fischer, *Stalin and German Communism*, 176.
14. Ibid., 174–75.
15. Quoted in Helmut Gruber, *International Communism in the Era of Lenin* (New York: Anchor Books, 1972), 306.
16. Borkenau, *World Communism*, 214.
17. Fischer, *Stalin and German Communism*, 175.
18. Quoted in Borkenau, *World Communism*, 216.
19. Quoted in Degras, vol. 1, 225.
20. *Decisions of the Third Congress of the Communist International* (London: Communist Party of Great Britain, 1921), 18.
21. Quoted in Degras, *Communist International*, vol. 1, 311.
22. Ibid., 317–19.
23. Trotsky, *First Five Years*, vol. 2, 91–95. Emphases in the original.
24. Lenin, *Collected Works*, vol. 33, 430.
25. Ibid., 65–66.
26. Degras, *Communist International*, vol. 1, 425. The question of what precisely this meant remained a matter of dispute between left and right in the International. For Trotsky the "workers' government" was "a form of proletarian dictatorship." The *Theses,* however, explicitly endorsed participation in "a government of workers and the poorer peasants...possible in the Balkans, Czechoslovakia, Poland, etc." and in the undefined and extremely elastic category of "workers' governments in which

communists participate." But what were they, as opposed to "the real workers' government...which consists of communists"?

27. Degras, *Communist International*, vol. 1, 427.
28. Quoted in ibid., 425–26.
29. Ibid., 426.
30. Trotsky, *First Five Years*, vol. 2, 127–28. The *Journal du Peuple* was a paper run as a personal venture, with a centrist line, by Henri Fabre, a Communist Party member whom Frossard and others were trying to protect from expulsion.
31. Carr, *Bolshevik Revolution*, vol. 3, 416.
32. Borkenau, *World Communism*, 228.
33. A. F. Upton, *The Communist Parties of Scandinavia and Finland* (London: Weidenfeld and Nicolson, 1973), 481.
34. Braunthal, *History of International*, vol. 2, 156.
35. Ibid., 241.
36. Ibid., 246–47.
37. Ibid., 175, note.
38. Quoted in Degras, *Communist International*, vol. 1, 171.
39. Carr, *Bolshevik Revolution*, vol. 3, 397.
40. Quoted in E. H. Carr, *Socialism in One Country* (London: Penguin Books. 1972), vol. 3, 575.
41. Ibid., 545.
42. Ibid., 554.
43. Quoted in Degras, *Communist International*, vol. 1, 415–16.
44. Degras, *Communist International*, vol. 1, 412.

Chapter 4: 1923: The Crucial Year

1. E. H. Carr, *The Interregnum 1923–24* (London: Penguin Books, 1969), 5.
2. Lenin, *Collected Works*, vol. 33, 279.
3. Leon Trotsky, *The Challenge of the Left Opposition (1928–29)* (New York: Pathfinder Press, 1981), 202–203.
4. Carr, *Interregnum*, 198.
5. Quoted in Ibid., 198.
6. Ibid., 199.
7. Lenin, *Collected Works*, vol. 25, 286–89; emphasis in the original.
8. Quoted in Carr, *Interregnum*, 200.
9. Quoted in Helmut Gruber, *International Communism in the Era of Lenin: A Documentary History* (Greenwich, Conn: Fawcett Publications, 1967), 169–60.
10. Evelyn Anderson, *Hammer or Anvil?* (London: Victor Gollancz, 1945), 87.
11. Quoted in Borkenau, *Wolrd Communism*, 236.

12. Harman, *Lost Revolution*, 223. Chapters 11, 12, and 13 of this book are essential reading on the German October.

13. Robert Wohl, *French Communism in the Making* (Stanford CA: Stanford University Press, 1966), 319–20.

14. This was the so-called "Schlageter agitation." See Harman, *Lost Revolution,* 252–54.

15. Quoted in Harman, *Lost Revolution*, 260.

16. Quoted in Carr, *Interregnum*, 195.

17. Carr, *Interregnum*, 209.

18. The French communist Albert, quoted in Harman, *Lost Revolution*, 292.

19. "Letter to Thalheimer," quoted in ibid., 284.

20. Trotsky, "Through what stage are we passing?" in *Challenge of the Left Opposition (1923–1925)* (New York: Pathfinder Press, 1975).

21. Lenin, *Collected Works*, vol. 33, 288–89.

22. Ibid., 288.

23. Quoted in Carr, *Interregnum*, 365.

24. Trotsky, *The Revolution Betrayed* (London: New Park Publications, 1967), 212.

Chapter 5: Left Oscillation—Right Turn 1924–1928

1. Degras, *Communist International*, vol. 2, 77–78.

2. Trotsky, *The Third International after Lenin* (New York: Pioneer Publishers, 1936), 100.

3. Isaac Deutscher, "The Tragedy of the Polish Communist Party" in *Marxism in Our Time* (London: Cape, 1972), 123.

4. Lenin, *Collected Works*, vol. 25, 385; emphasis in the original.

5. See Degras, *Communist International*, vol. 2, 151–52.

6. Quoted in Carr, *Socialism in One Country*, vol. 3, 85.

7. Ibid., 85.

8. Ibid., 305; emphasis in the original.

9. Borkenau, *World Communism*, 263.

10. Carr, *Socialism in One Country*, vol. 3, 410.

11. Quoted in ibid., 296.

12. Trotsky, *Third International after Lenin*, 125.

13. Carr, *Socialism in One Country*, vol. 1, 194.

14. Quoted in Carr, *Interregnum*, 267.

15. Carr, *Socialism in One Country*, vol. 3, 215–16.

16. Trotsky, *Third International after Lenin*, 120.

17. Quoted in ibid., 120–21.

18. Theodore Draper, *American Communism and Soviet Russia* (New York: Viking Press, 1960), 43–44.

19. Ibid., 48.

20. Deutscher, "Tragedy of Polish Communist," 125–26.
21. Ibid., 135–36.
22. See Duncan Hallas and Chris Harman, *Days of Hope: The General Strike of 1926* (London: Socialists Unlimited, 1981) for a brief account.
23. Degras, *Communist International*, vol. 2, 260–61.
24. Brian Pearce, "Early Years of the CPGB" in Michael Woodhouse and Brian Pearce, *History of Communism in Britain* (London: New Park Publications, 1975), 165.
25. Carr, *Socialism in One Country*, vol. 3, 597.
26. Nigel Harris, *The Mandate of Heaven: Marx and Mao in Modern China* (London: Quartet Books, 1978), 5.
27. Degras, *Communist International*, vol. 2, 9.
28. Harold Isaacs, *The Tragedy of the Chinese Revolution* (New York: Octagon Books, 1968), 70.
29. Quoted in Harris, *Mandate of Heaven*, 9.
30. Quoted in K. Tilak, *The Rise and Fall of the Comintern* (Bombay: Spark Syndicate, 1947), 33.
31. Quoted in Isaacs, *Tragedy of Chinese Revolution*, 117.

Chapter 6: The Third Period 1928–1934

1. E. H. Carr, *The Russian Revolution from Lenin to Stalin* (London: Macmillan, 1980), 124.
2. These figures and those that follow are from Allen Nove, *An Economic History of the USSR* (London: Pelican Books, 1972). The figures have been rounded to the nearest half of one percent.
3. Quoted in Degras, *Communist International*, vol. 2, 456.
4. Ibid., vol. 3, 44.
5. E. H. Carr, *Foundations of a Planned Economy*, vol. 3, part 2 (London: Macmillan, 1976), 415.
6. Carr, *The Twilight of the Comintern* (London: Macmillan, 1982), 178, 67.
7. Alastair Davidson, *The Communist Party of Australia* (Stanford, CA: Stanford University Press, 1969), 53, 61.
8. Carr, *Twilight of Comintern*, 51.
9. Anderson, *Hammer or Anvil?*, 131.
10. Ibid., 135–36.
11. Trotsky, *The Struggle against Fascism in Germany* (New York: Citadel Press, 1971), 155–56. (Emphasis added.)
12. Quoted in Carr, *Twilight of Comintern*, 25.
13. Ibid., 26.
14. Trotsky, *Struggle against Fascism*, 59 and following.
15. Anderson, *Hammer or Anvil?*, 147–48.
16. Degras, *Communist International*, vol. 3, 213.

17. Borkenau, *World Communism*, 364.
18. Quoted in Carr, *Socialism in One Country*, vol. 3, 86.
19. Trotsky, *Struggle against Fascism*, 157.
20. Quoted in Carr, *Twilight of Comintern*, 29.
21. Trotsky, *Struggle against Fascism*, 342.

Chapter 7: The Terror and the People's Front

1. Central Committee of the CPSU, *History of the Communist Party of the Soviet Union (Bolshevik)* (New York: International Publishers, 1939), 319.
2. Nikita Khrushchev, *The Secret Speech* (Nottingham: Spokesman Books, 1976), 33.
3. Quoted in Degras, *Communist International*, vol. 3, 375.
4. Quoted inTom Kemp, *Stalinism in France*, vol. 1 (London: New Park Publications, 1983), 118.
5. Degras, *Communist International*, vol. 3, 384.
6. E. H. Carr, *The Comintern and the Spanish Civil War* (London: Macmillan, 1984), 3.
7. Quoted in Felix Morrow, *Revolution and Counterrevolution in Spain* (London: New Park Publications, 1963), 34.
8. Pierre Broué and Emile Témime, *The Revolution and Civil War in Spain* (London: Faber, 1972), 127.
9. Hugh Thomas, *The Civil War in Spain* (London: Penguin Books, 1965), 796.
10. Burnett Bolloten, *The Grand Camouflage* (London: Hollis and Carter, 1961), 81–86.
11. This is described in detail in Felix Morrow's book.
12. Quoted in Degras, *Communist International*, vol. 3, 439.
13. Ibid., 443–44. (Emphasis added.)
14. Ibid., 472.
15. Fernando Claudin, *The Communist Movement* (London: Penguin Books, 1975), 45.
16. Vladimir Dedijer, *Tito Speaks* (London: Weidenfeld and Nicolson, 1953), 391.

Chapter 8: The Legacy of the Comintern

1. Tony Cliff's *Lenin*, especially vols. 1 and 2, convincingly demonstrates this.
2. Claudin, *Communist Movement*, 107–108.
3. Lenin, *Collected Works*, vol. 21, 31.
4. Trotsky, *My Life*, 249.
5. See Ian Birchall, *Workers Against the Monolith* (London: Pluto Press, 1974).

CHRONOLOGY

1889

Second International formed at the Congress of Paris.

1907

Stuttgart Congress of the Second International unanimously adopts resolution against war.

1914

August: Start of First World War. German and Austrian Social Democratic Parties, French Socialist Party, British and Belgian Labor Parties all vote support for their national governments in the war.

November: Lenin writes: "The Second International is dead.... Long live the Third International."

1915

September: International socialist antiwar conference at Zimmerwald.

1916

April: International socialist antiwar conference at Kienthal. Easter Rising in Dublin.

June: 50,000 Berlin workers strike as Karl Liebknecht is tried for organizing a peace demonstration.

1917

February (old calendar): Tsar overthrown in Russia.

April: 200,000 German metalworkers strike over bread ration. Independent Social Democratic Party of Germany (USPD) formed.

September: International socialist antiwar conference at Stockholm.

October (old calendar): Bolshevik revolution in Russia.

1918

January: Wave of antiwar strikes in Austria, Hungary, and Germany.

November: Naval mutiny and revolution in Germany ends war and leaves government in the hands of an SPD/USPD Council of People's Commissars.

December: German Communist Party (KPD) formed.

1919

January: Spartakus Rising in Berlin—Rosa Luxemburg and Karl Liebknecht murdered. Summons to first congress of Communist International issued from Moscow.

February: Berne conference of parties of the Second International.

March: First, founding congress of the Comintern in Moscow. Hungarian soviet republic established.

April: Bavarian Soviet Republic established.

May: Bavarian Soviet Republic crushed.

June/July: Semi-insurrectionary riots over food prices in Italy.

August: Hungarian soviet republic crushed.

September: Bologna Congress of the Italian Socialist Party (PSI) votes by a large majority to support its executive's decision to join the Comintern.

October: Heidelberg Congress of KPD expels ultralefts.

November: General election in Italy: PSI gains nearly one-third of the vote.

1920

March: Kapp Putsch in Germany.

April: General strike in Turin region of Italy to defend factory councils.

July: International Trade Union Council formed in Moscow to organize international congress of Red trade unions.

July/August: Second Congress of Comintern. Geneva Congress of Second International.

September: Occupation of the factories in Italy. Baku Congress of Eastern Peoples.

October: Halle Congress of USPD votes to affiliate to Comintern.

December: Tours Congress of French Socialist Party votes to affiliate to Comintern.

1921

January: Livorno Congress of Italian Socialist Party refuses to expel reformists: left wing splits away to form Italian Communist Party (PCI).

February: Vienna conference of parties that have left the Second International but not joined the Comintern forms the Vienna or "Two-and-a-half" International.

March: March Action in Germany. Introduction of New Economic Policy (NEP) in Russia.

June/July: Third Congress of Comintern.

July: First congress of Red International of Labor Unions (RILU or Profintern) in Moscow.

December: Executive committee of Comintern issues directives on united front.

1922

April: Meeting of representatives of Third, Second, and "Two-and-a-half" Internationals in Berlin.

October: "March on Rome" brings Mussolini to power in Italy.

November/December: Fourth Congress of Comintern.

1923

January: French and Belgian troops occupy the Ruhr.

May: Hamburg congress reunites Second and "Two-and-a-half" Internationals as "Labor and Socialist International."

June: Right-wing coup overthrows Peasant Party government in Bulgaria.

September: Abortive Communist Party insurrection in Bulgaria.

October: German Communist Party calls off planned insurrection. Open Letter written by Trotsky begins Left Opposition in Russia.

November: General strike in Poland—workers seize Krakow.

1924

January: Death of Lenin.

May: Thirteenth congress of Communist Party of the Soviet Union (CPSU) confirms troika of Zinoviev, Kamenev, and Stalin in power.

June/July: Fifth congress of Comintern.

December: Abortive Communist Party uprising in Reval, Estonia.

1925

March: Fifth plenum of the Comintern Executive declares "The period of revolutionary upsurge has ended."

April: Sofia Cathedral in Bulgaria bombed by Communist Party's military section. Formation of Anglo-Soviet Trade Union Committee in Britain.

May/June: General strike in Shanghai, China, spreading to other cities.

December: Fourteenth congress of CPSU—Zinoviev and Kamenev defeated. End of Zinoviev's dominance of the Comintern.

1926

March: Chiang Kai-shek launches military coup against Chinese Communist Party in Canton.

May: Pilsudski coup in Poland. General strike in Britain.

July: United Opposition of Trotsky, Zinoviev, and Kamenev formed.

1927

April: Kuomintang massacres Chinese Communist Party members in Shanghai.

November: Trotsky expelled from CPSU.

December: Abortive Communist Party rising in Canton, China.

1928

July/August: Sixth congress of Comintern—"Third Period" proclaimed. End of Bukharin's dominance of the Comintern.

1929

May: First Five-Year Plan launched in Russia.

July: Tenth plenum of Comintern Executive revives theory of "social fascism."

October: Wall Street crash in USA.

1930

September: Elections in Germany—Nazi vote shoots up from 1928 total of 800,000 to 6,400,000.

1933

January: Hitler comes to power in Germany.

1934

January: Seventeenth congress of CPSU proclaims "the victory of socialism" in Russia.

February: French fascists march on Chamber of Deputies, prompting big united antifascist demonstrations. Austrian socialists suppressed and military dictatorship established under Dolfuss.

1935

July/August: Seventh congress of Comintern.

1936

June: Popular Front wins elections in France. Wave of factory occupations.

July: Military coup in Spain halted by workers' uprising. Start of Spanish Civil War.

August: Start of Moscow show trials.

1939

August: Hitler-Stalin Pact.

September: Start of Second World War.

1941

June: Germany invades Russia.

1943

May: Comintern dissolved.

INDEX

ABOUT HAYMARKET BOOKS

Haymarket Books is a nonprofit, progressive book distributor and publisher, a project of the Center for Economic Research and Social Change. We believe that activists need to take ideas, history, and politics into the many struggles for social justice today. Learning the lessons of past victories, as well as defeats, can arm a new generation of fighters for a better world. As Karl Marx said, "The philosophers have merely interpreted the world; the point, however, is to change it."

We take inspiration and courage from our namesakes, the Haymarket Martyrs, who gave their lives fighting for a better world. Their 1886 struggle for the eight-hour day, which gave us May Day, the international workers' holiday, reminds workers around the world that ordinary people can organize and struggle for their own liberation. These struggles continue today across the globe—struggles against oppression, exploitation, hunger, and poverty.

It was August Spies, one of the Martyrs who was targeted for being an immigrant and an anarchist, who predicted the battles being fought to this day. "If you think that by hanging us you can stamp out the labor movement," Spies told the judge, "then hang us. Here you will tread upon a spark, but here, and there, and behind you, and in front of you, and everywhere, the flames will blaze up. It is a subterranean fire. You cannot put it out. The ground is on fire upon which you stand."

We could not succeed in our publishing efforts without the generous financial support of our readers. Many people contribute to our project through the Haymarket Sustainers program, where donors receive free books in return for their monetary support. If you would like to be a part of this program, please contact us at info@haymarketbooks.org.

Order these titles and more online at
www.haymarketbooks.org or call 773-583-7884.

CPSIA information can be obtained
at www.ICGtesting.com
Printed in the USA
LVHW081102020321
680315LV00004B/4